Woman of Grace

A Titus 2 Mentoring Program

ANNE BROWN

CROSS to CROWN
MINISTRIES

Comments from Participants

I could do this once a week for the rest of my life! ~ Linda

I've always wanted to be a godly Christian wife and mother, but I never knew how. Now I know what it looks like, and I can work toward putting it into practice in my life. ~ Rebecca

I felt so loved and pampered every week! ~ Deb

I loved the practical application of how to be a godly wife. I could go home and apply the things I learned. Not every woman grew up in a Christian home with a good model to follow, so this class shows women how to be godly wives and mothers. ~ Stacy

This program is a biblical model and "living out" of Titus 2. More women need to be taught the role that God has for them. ~ Rosa

I enjoyed getting to know the mentors; it was comforting knowing they are not perfect. As they shared their mistakes and lessons learned, it was nice to know I don't have to hide my flaws. ~ Julie

This program is invaluable because husbands and children don't come with "how-to" manuals. You bring the Bible's instructions for us to life. ~ Jeanie

When the mentors teach, it helps us as younger women because we are just beginning this chapter of marriage and raising kids. The mentors apply Titus 2 directly in their lives which is such a great example to us. ~ Tamara

This was such a wonderful experience, I cannot tell you how much each mentor meant to me personally. They each brought a very special piece of themselves each week that filled my heart with joy, anticipation, and excitement. Their love and devotion to our Lord was such an encouragement to me. ~ Megan

This program has changed my life and was one of the best things that ever happened to me. It changed my attitude toward my family and made me realize they are worth the effort! I discovered that my family deserved a home that was clean, and they deserved to know where their clean clothes were. I stopped thinking of those things as chores that had to be done, and started thinking of them as ways I could bless my family. I found that by making time to give my husband and children a well-run home suddenly I had more time to do the fun things. In my case, I chose to spend one day each week to do it all. I think also realizing that other women had struggled with all the topics we discussed helped me feel more like I could face my faults and deal with them. ~ Courtney

I loved the opportunity to develop relationships with the other women and glean from the mentors. I loved hearing about their "been there/done that" experiences - all with Christian principles and guidelines. One of the most important things I learned about "loving my husband" is that he is a higher priority than my kids. I sometimes give all my energy to my kids, cleaning, cooking, "working out," etc. so that I am crabby and exhausted by the time he wants/needs me to be his friend, companion, listener and lover. ~ Cami

The day you meet is my wife's favorite day of the week! She can hardly wait until you meet each week. ~ A husband

Oftentimes we are expected to know how to do things in our role as wife/mom but are never taught how to do them. This program provides a safe place to learn and be encouraged. ~ Jillian

It is so important today in our culture to hear from women who are wise and experienced in their Christian life. I felt very "loved on" and I appreciate the relationships built with the mentors. ~ Ruth Ann

I am so grateful for our mentors. These are strong godly women who live out today's "Proverbs 31 woman." It's good for me to see those who have walked the road longer (and are still walking)... their advice, laughter, wisdom, etc. I loved coming into a home of fun, honest, loving and godly women every week. I was refreshed and renewed every time we met. ~ Julie

Woman of Grace: A Titus 2 Mentoring Program
Copyright © 2014 by Anne Brown
Published by Cross to Crown Ministries, Colorado Springs, CO 80919

ISBN: 978-0-9851187-5-4

Cover by Erin McLaughlin

Printed in the United States of America.

To Dwight, the love of my life,

My loving husband, the wonderful father of our three sons,

My best friend and confidante, my spiritual leader, my encourager,

My pastor and teacher over decades of ministry together.

Contents

Acknowledgements

I first want to thank my Lord and Savior Jesus Christ for His marvelous salvation, bestowed on me so graciously in my first year of marriage in Lincoln, Nebraska. I thank Him for His Word which instructs believers in following Him, and the Spirit who guides, teaches, and instructs us in the path of righteousness.

Thanks also to my faithful and loving husband Dwight who has always encouraged me to use my Spiritual gifts throughout our ministry over the years. Thanks too for his putting up with endless meetings and teaching sessions that have interrupted our household and his schedule over the years. If he had not bought me my own computer three years ago, this project would not have been possible.

Thanks to Beth Wahl who first encouraged me to write a new and updated mentoring program and to write a book that could be shared with other churches and ministries in their quest for mentoring women.

Thanks to Carol Wood and Debbie Merritt who helped in the re-writing of several of the lessons and continued to encourage me in this endeavor.

Thanks to Alicia Reeves who did all of the layout and beautiful illustrations for the documents which eventually became this book. Her talent is remarkable!

Thanks to Doug and Krista Goodin for all of their editing help and careful documenting of the quotes in the manuscript.

Thanks to my principle mentoring team over the last few years—Carol Wood, Debbie Merritt, and Pam Shannon. Their encouragement, prayers, and help have been a testimony of their devotion to the admonition of Titus 2:3-5 and of their desire to be obedient to the command of Scripture. They have faithfully used their Spiritual gifts to encourage and strengthen young married women in their marriages and walk with the Lord. I also thank them for their willingness to give both of their time and finances to minister each year in instructing the young women of our church. They have regularly shared their own failures and successes in life and marriage to help others marvel at the wonderful work of God. Finally, Pam, our culinary chef extraordinaire, constantly challenges those of us less talented in our cooking endeavors to "excel still more" in that area of our lives. Thank you!

Foreword

As a pastor's wife for many years, I was actively involved in women's lives through teaching Bible studies and Sunday school, writing devotionals, and leading special events in our various churches. But it wasn't until years later that I heard a familiar voice on *Focus on the Family* talking about the importance of not just teaching women but *mentoring* them. That voice was Vickie Kraft, a former teacher of mine, advertising her program *Heart to Heart*. In that moment, I was introduced to the concept of building relationships while studying Scripture together. That concept has changed my life. It has become my passion. Since then, I have been involved in many different approaches to mentoring, including the marriage/mothering/home-keeping program based on Titus 2:3-5 that you now hold in your hands. Through it, I have seen changed lives, saved marriages, and young women encouraged not only in their walk with the Lord, but also in their personal character and relationships within their families.

Many women today did not grow up in Christian homes and never had a good role model to follow as they moved from their single lives into marriage. In other cases, they (or their mothers) were just too busy or not interested in passing wisdom and knowledge from mother to daughter. Young wives need help both spiritually and practically for their roles in life.

Some churches or other Christian groups talk about the need for mentoring women, but few are intentional in carrying it out. It takes more than talk. Without a plan, it usually will not happen. *Woman of Grace* is a program ready-made to help you!

It is a short, seven-week study followed by a celebration dinner for the graduates. Keeping it relatively short is helpful in recruiting mentors – they don't have to commit for a semester or a whole year. Mentors meet for three-hour segments with the young women: one hour for cooking, one hour for study, and one hour for eating around a table and discussing how to put into practice what they have studied.

This book also includes some of our favorite recipes and a manual entitled *Called to Mentor* that can be used to prepare your mentors for their mentoring responsibilities. These lessons can also be used in group settings or in one-on-one studies.

It is my prayer that this program will be used to prepare our next generation of wives and mothers both spiritually and practically to become women of grace who will serve their families well, radiate Christian character, and bring honor and glory to the name of our Lord Jesus.

Anne Brown
Colorado Springs
2014

WOMANOFGRACE

An excellent wife, who can find? For her worth is far above jewels.

Christ Calls Us to Keep Our Homes

An excellent wife who can find? For her worth is far above jewels...she looks well to the ways of her household and does not eat the bread of idleness. Her children rise up and bless her, her husband also praises her...give her the product of her hands and let her works praise her in the gates. (Proverbs 31)

Practicing grace by being content at home, serving our families as a ministry to them because we love Jesus.

Introduction

Likewise, teach the older women to be reverent in the way they live, not to be slanderers or addicted to much wine, but to teach what is good. Then they can train the younger women to love their husbands and children, to be self-controlled and pure, to be busy at home, to be kind, and to be subject to their husbands, so that no one will malign the word of God. (Titus 2:3-5 NIV)

The apostle Paul wrote these words to Titus, a young pastor he left on the island of Crete to organize the churches through appointing elders and giving instructions for godly living to the older and younger church members. Because the Cretan citizens were known as "liars, evil beasts, and lazy gluttons," the older women needed to learn good Christian behavior. They, in turn, could train the younger women how to love their husbands and children, take care of their households, and demonstrate godly character to the world around them.

The fact that the older women were instructed to teach the younger women demonstrates that these disciplines don't necessarily come easily to all young women. But they *can* be taught. Younger women can learn to live their lives pleasing to the Lord so that "no one will malign the word of God." That is the ultimate goal of this instruction.

The phrase "be busy at home" is the Greek word *oikourgos*. It is a compound word from the two root words: *oikos* (a dwelling, home, household) and *ergon* (to work or to be employed). It speaks of working at home, domestic duties, or managing the home. This title implies that a woman is to be diligent, working hard to run her household. She has a unique opportunity to guard its influences and atmosphere. She is able to monitor what comes in and goes out of her home for the benefit and blessing of her husband and family. Her activities as the home manager allow her the freedom and creativity to express her love and care for her family, along with establishing an environment in which each family member can thrive. Keeping a household running smoothly is a goal that all of us can strive to achieve. And it is a major biblical emphasis in the God-given ministry of the wife.

Have you ever thought of homemaking as a *ministry*? God thinks it is! A wife's home and family are her sphere of influence where she creatively serves both God and her family. Like all ministries, the administrative and domestic skills involved in managing a household take planning and perseverance. As she strives for excellence, she will experience the satisfaction of blessing others.

In her book *A Woman's High Calling*, Elizabeth George exhorts women to remember that "home is where your heart is...just be there!" She continues to share some basic truths:

> "Home is the hub...of constructive activity, loving family relationships, and the many good things in life."
>
> "Home is a haven...a safe place. It's a harbor and a port where vessels and wayfarers find shelter. And shouldn't our homes offer such shelter and safety to our cherished family?"
>
> "Home is a hospital...to two different needs that our precious family members experience...." These include the physical and the emotional.
>
> "Home is to be happy...as home managers and homemakers, [you] have the job assignment of providing the home magic and the homemade medicine of 'happiness.'" In other words, the mother sets the tone for the day and the family's time at home.
>
> "Home is a hearth. In days gone by...it was the center of the home." Home should be a place where the family members gather together to feel warmth and get nourishment.

"Home is for hospitality…to minister not only to family but also to strangers who need a 'hotel,' a hearth, a haven, a hospital…it is our privilege to extend such love to outsiders…."[1]

How each woman carries out her activities in the home will vary depending on her circumstances and stage of life. There is no one-size-fits-all pattern that everyone must follow. For example, women working outside the home will have a different way of doing things from a mom at home caring for young children. Whatever your situation, you and your husband need to agree on how the household should run, with all family members carefully considering their responsibilities.

Being a keeper at home is a high calling which, by God's grace, serves your family well.

Biblical Foundation

An excellent wife, who can find? For her worth is far above jewels. The heart of her husband trusts in her, and he will have no lack of gain. She does him good and not evil all the days of her life. She looks for wool and flax and works with her hands in delight. She is like merchant ships; she brings her food from afar. She rises also while it is still night and gives food to her household and portions to her maidens. She considers a field and buys it; from her earnings she plants a vineyard. She girds herself with strength and makes her arms strong. She senses that her gain is good; her lamp does not go out at night. She stretches out her hands to the distaff, and her hands grasp the spindle. She extends her hand to the poor, and she stretches out her hands to the needy. She is not afraid of the snow for her household, for all her household are clothed with scarlet. She makes coverings for herself; her clothing is fine linen and purple. Her husband is known in the gates, when he sits among the elders of the land. She makes linen garments and sells them, and supplies belts to the tradesmen. Strength and dignity are her clothing, and she smiles at the future. She opens her mouth in wisdom, and the teaching of kindness is on her tongue. She looks well to the ways of her household, and does not eat the bread of idleness. Her children rise up and bless her; her husband also, and he praises her, saying: "Many daughters have done nobly, but you excel them all." Charm is deceitful and beauty is vain, but a woman who fears the Lord, she shall be praised. Give her the product of her hands, and let her works praise her in the gates. (Proverbs 31:10-31)

Use the chart on the next page to list your answers to the following questions:

- What tasks or activities does the Proverbs 31 woman do?

- What character traits does she demonstrate in those activities?

Activities	Character Traits

- Which of the activities listed do you also do?

- What other responsibilities do you have in your home?

- What is one household project you would like to complete or learn?

- With what skills do you need help?

    ☐ Bill paying/financial management/budgeting

    ☐ Cleaning

    ☐ Home decorating

    ☐ Sewing/mending

    ☐ Laundry

    ☐ Cooking/meal planning

    ☐ Home organization

    ☐ Grocery shopping

    ☐ Gardening

- What one thing could you resolve to change or improve as a result of this lesson?

Planning & Organization

The Proverbs 31 woman was prepared for the future. She made plans for the day, contemplating her family's needs in advance.

Organize your individual days and weeks in advance. Either think in blocks of time or use your calendar to plan your schedule for the coming week. Many people find it helpful to make a list of chores or activities to be done each day. The more organized you are, the more you will accomplish. Years ago I heard of the *$10,000 Plan*. There was a prominent businessman who was totally unorganized. Because he was desperate, he offered a prize of $10,000 to anyone that could help him get organized. This was the plan:

- Make a list of all you have to accomplish for the day.

- Place the items in a priority order with those that *must* be done first at the top of the list. Next, list those jobs that are the hardest or that you don't like to do. Finally, list other items that can be done in smaller amounts of time (e.g., in fifteen minute blocks). Projects that are not completed on the specified day are brought over to the next day to accomplish.

- Cross each item off your list as you complete it. (This is not part of the original plan, but I added it because it gives me *so much pleasure* to cross items off my list. It makes me feel like I have accomplished so much.)

Here are some tips to plan ahead for the needs of your family:

1. Keep enough food on hand so that you can prepare nutritious meals and snacks. Plan weekly menus ahead of time so that you won't have to go back to the store for forgotten items. When cooking, make a double batch of what you are preparing and freeze half to be used at another time. If you have pantry space, keep additional staples of foods you use regularly.

2. Have a plan so that your family can keep up with the laundry.

3. Plan ahead for clothing purchases for your family. At the end of the season, you can anticipate what clothing needs your family will have for the following year and buy them at clearance prices. Shop at thrift shops, garage sales, and consignment swap meets to find gently worn clothes. Graciously accept hand-me-down clothes from family members and friends. (This is recycling among friends.)

4. Keep a list in a convenient place where you write down items that must be purchased at the store. When you run out of a product or are nearing the time it must be replaced, write it on the list. (Don't run out of toilet paper, for example.) Teach your family to tell you when they need supplies, so it can be added to your list.

A few more helpful hints:

1. Habitually put things in the same place. You will always know where they are and it will help keep your home organized. As an example, hang up jackets and coats and have a place to put your keys.

2. Try to handle mail and email only once. Throw it away/delete it or file it where it goes. Keep folders for important documents. Know where bills and receipts should be stored.

3. Teach your children to put their own toys, books, and clothing away. Help them to organize their closet and room so that they have space for their possessions. Provide a toy chest or storage container for their things. Place hangers for coats and clothes at a level that they can reach. Place a crate or a tub for shoes and boots near the doors where the family comes in.

4. Get up earlier than the rest of the family and ask God to bless your day. Read a short devotional for the day. Dedicate your day to the Lord. Get ready for it and the entire day will be much less frantic.

5. In the evening, think about your next day. For example, set out clothing for you and your children.

Finances

Finances often cause stress in the family. It is important for you and your husband to establish a budget based on your needs and income. It will, of necessity, vary from time to time due to job changes, the number of children in the family, and large expenses such as a home, car, health needs, etc. Much prayer and planning must be done together to meet the challenges facing young families today. John MacArthur gave an interesting illustration regarding finances:

> "Imagine a couple…that didn't operate on a margin, and as so many couples did, they followed the great American way…You buy the things you don't need with money you don't have from the people you don't even like. And so they get themselves in a situation where they are overextended. They have more obligations than they do income…Along the way, they've taken under their wing the support of their local church and perhaps some friends who've gone to the mission field. What happens?
>
> Well, pretty soon, they find they can't meet that missionary's need. And pretty soon they can't give to the local ministry what God has designed in their own life for them to give. And then maybe they get to the place where they face bankruptcy. The loss of the car, the loss of the house, the loss of the job, and the loss of the testimony. And now they are limited as to what they can do for God, because they are having to pay for their foolishness with every dime they get. If God ever came to them and called them away to some mission field, they couldn't go."[2]

You must seek God's help to live within your family budget. Also, take advantage of the many Christian resources available to help you manage your finances.

Questions to ask:

- Am I content with the standard of living that I enjoy now?

- If my budget is too tight, how can I help to cut family expenses?

- Am I living in such a way that there is money available for Kingdom use?

- How do I look at my money and resources?

Meal Planning

Use a meal planning chart to plan ahead of time. List all of the food items you will need for each meal. Add the regular items you buy every week (milk, bread, juice, fruit, etc.) to a shopping list. Don't grocery shop when you're hungry!

Grocery Shopping

Careful grocery shopping is a skill that can be developed over the years. It is helpful to plan each week's meals *before* you go to the grocery store. By planning ahead, you will be able to make fewer trips to the store. Things to consider: *How much money do I have to spend on groceries per week? Will my husband or children need to take lunches to school or work? Will we be entertaining guests during the week or taking a meal to another family? When can we eat leftovers during the week? Are there any nights when we will not be eating at home this week?*

Ways to save money during grocery shopping:

1. Plan your meals by buying fruits and vegetables that are seasonal and on sale.

2. Check your local paper or the internet to find sale items for that week. Sales usually run weekly. Check blogs for seasonal recipes.

3. Use coupons if you have time. Some stores double coupons which adds to your savings. Some stores have coupons on the store shelves for customers to use. Check for rebates on items that you use.

4. Try store brands and see if you like them. Some are manufactured by the same companies that make the major brands.

5. Shop farmers' markets for local, fresh produce. Form a food co-op with friends or join an existing one.

6. Plant a garden.

7. Choose stores that are convenient and carry the items you buy regularly.

8. Check your receipts before leaving the store.

9. Watch for sales on staples that you use regularly. Pick up extras if you have storage space. Shop at stores that have BOGO (buy one, get one free) events.

Household Care & Cleaning

Plan, with your husband's input, the household cleaning, chores, and yard work that need to be done daily, weekly, monthly, or seasonally. This will vary from family to family according to your stages of life and changing expectations. However, providing a clean house (minimizing germs, dirt, and mold), will help keep your family healthier. Keeping clutter under control will help prevent household accidents and reduce stress.

Before you go to bed, finish cleaning the kitchen and pick up clutter and toys so that you are ready for the next day. Give children age-appropriate household chores as they grow up. Teach them responsibility for their jobs and that they are a part of a team called "the family."

Summary

We cannot say it better than Carolyn Mahaney:

> So I have made this my prayer: "Lord, help me to build the kind of home where all who enter find it 'impossible to keep from thinking of God'."[3]

Prayer

Lord, give me a heart for my family. Help me to create an environment where they will grow physically, emotionally, mentally, and spiritually. May I see their needs as an opportunity of service to my family. Help me to remember that all I do is to be done to glorify God and should be given my very best effort. Thank you, Lord, that you have entrusted these loved ones into my care. May I view their care as a sacred ministry from you. May Christ enable me each day to serve you in this way. Amen.

Notes

[1] Elizabeth George, *A Woman's High Calling*, (Eugene, OR: Harvest House Publishers, 2001), pp. 251-259.

[2] John MacArthur, "The Christian and His Finances," *Grace to You* broadcast, December 30, 1973.

[3] Carolyn Mahaney, *Feminine Appeal* (Wheaton, IL: Crossway, 2003), p.114.

WOMAN OF GRACE **WEEKLY MENU PLANNER**

	Breakfast	Lunch	Dinner
Sunday			
Monday			
Tuesday			
Wednesday			
Thursday			
Friday			
Saturday			

WOMANOFGRACE

The fruit of the Spirit is love, joy, peace, patience, kindness...

Christ Calls Us to Kindness

Be kind to one another, tender-hearted, forgiving each other, just as God in Christ also has forgiven you. (Ephesians 4:32)

Practicing grace by showing kindness to those whom God brings into our lives.

Introduction

Kindness means being sympathetic, friendly, gentle, tender-hearted, or generous.

Titus 2:3-5 teaches us that the older women are to teach the younger women the attribute of kindness. It is essential that kindness is at the core of our being. We cannot love our husband or children, have the desire for purity in our marriage, or have consistent moral excellence without kindness. It is the key to love – "We love, because He first loved us." (1 John 4:19). Kindness is neither natural nor normal in our society, so it must be taught. In *Bringing Up Girls*, Dr. James Dobson writes an entire chapter on bullying behavior among girls. "Girls [bully] relationally, by backstabbing, harassing, name-calling, isolating, spreading rumors and lies, and just being nasty. Taunting behavior of this ilk is pervasive wherever girls are found."[1] Mean girls are everywhere, even in starring roles of movies, TV shows, and tabloids.

Often, marriages suffer because one party is unkind or mean and the other responds out of anger and hurt. Tempers flare, harsh words fly, relationships are destroyed. Jesus came to earth as our perfect example of lovingkindness by sacrificing His life for us while we were yet sinners. Because He lives in us, we are free to respond with kindness rather than retaliation.

"Make sure that nobody pays back wrong for wrong, but always try to be kind to each other and to everyone else." (1 Thessalonians 5:15 NIV)

It is basic human nature to be nice to those who are nice to us. But we are a lot like children in a nursery. If no one messes with us or our stuff, we are unprovoked and there is peace. However, if one child takes a toy from another child, the second child will most likely grab the toy back. This encounter often escalates into one child hitting and the other child hitting back. Human nature protects "me" and "mine."

"Or do you show contempt for the riches of his kindness, tolerance and patience, not realizing that God's kindness leads you toward repentance?" (Romans 2:4 NIV)

There is a story about a woman who took this biblical truth to heart and saved a relationship with her husband. When he was being mean with his words toward her, she excused herself, got up from the couch and went to the kitchen to fix a snack of all his favorite foods and presented it to him on a fine plate. Instead of giving in to her own hurt and retaliating with unkind words, she overwhelmed him with lovingkindness. He apologized to her for being cruel with his words. Her kind response led him to repentance.

Jesus, of course, suffered the ultimate sacrifice. Kindness will mean our own sacrifice of time, personal comforts, personal rights, money, and energy.

Share a time when you counted the cost to be kind to someone or saw someone else do this.

Biblical Foundation

God commands us to be kind. Consider the following verses and meditate on the incredible kindness God bestowed on us by sending His one and only Son to die for us. This should make us desire to shower kindness on everyone else.

Be merciful, just as your Father is merciful. (Luke 6:36)

'Truly I say to you, to the extent that you did it to one of these brothers of Mine, even the least of them, you did it to Me.' (Matthew 25:40)

In everything, therefore, treat people the same way you want them to treat you. (Matthew 7:12)

Carry each other's burdens, and in this way you will fulfill the law of Christ. (Galatians 6:2 NIV)

Be kind to one another, tender-hearted, forgiving each other, just as God in Christ also has forgiven you. (Ephesians 4:32)

Honor all people, love the brotherhood, fear God, honor the king. (1 Peter 2:17)

May the Lord make your love increase and overflow for each other and for everyone else. (1 Thessalonians 3:12 NIV)

Make sure that nobody pays back wrong for wrong, but always try to be kind to each other and to everyone else. (1 Thessalonians 5:15 NIV)

- How can you apply these verses to a specific person in your life?

- Who would you consider the "least" in your life?

- What are ways that we may demonstrate respect to others?

The Difference Between Compassion and Kindness

Compassion is emotional sorrow for the troubles and sufferings of another, accompanied by an urge to help. Kindness, on the other hand, is the decision to do something to help someone else.

- Give an example of the difference between compassion and kindness.

An excellent example of biblical kindness is Dorcas (or Tabitha) in Acts 9:36-42:

Now in Joppa there was a disciple named Tabitha (which translated in Greek is called Dorcas); this woman was abounding with deeds of kindness and charity which she continually did. And it happened at that time that she fell sick and died; and when they had washed her body, they laid it in an upper room. Since Lydda was near Joppa, the disciples, having heard that Peter was there, sent two men to him, imploring him, "Do not delay in coming to us." So Peter arose and went with them. When he arrived, they brought him into the upper room; and all the widows stood beside him, weeping and showing all the tunics and garments that Dorcas used to make while she was with them. But Peter sent them all out and knelt down and prayed, and turning to the body, he said, "Tabitha, arise." And she opened her eyes, and when she saw Peter, she sat up. And he gave her his hand and raised her up; and calling the saints and widows, he presented her alive. It became known all over Joppa, and many believed in the Lord.

Dorcas modeled kindness in her deeds. Consider how her actions are pictured in each of these Scriptures:

Therefore, as we have opportunity, let us do good to all people, especially to those who belong to the family of believers. (Galatians 6:10 NIV)

Religion that God our Father accepts as pure and faultless is this: to look after orphans and widows in their distress and to keep oneself from being polluted by the world. (James 1:27 NIV)

For just as the body without the spirit is dead, so also faith without works is dead. (James 2:26)

Instruct them to do good, to be rich in good works, to be generous and ready to share. (1 Timothy 6:18)

Let your light shine before men in such a way that they may see your good works, and glorify your Father who is in heaven. (Matthew 5:16)

- How do our good works testify about our authentic faith?

- What deeds of kindness come to mind as you consider Dorcas' example?

- We don't often think about widows and orphans, but how may we minister to that specific group? How may this apply to single moms?

God will use our good works to not only benefit others, but also to bring glory to Himself. God can use our lives and our good deeds to draw men to salvation.

Kindness must be intentional, and it is a habit that can be developed.

Practical Examples for Developing a Habit of Kindness	
Notice the kindness of others throughout the day and be grateful. Look for simple acts like: • *Your spouse doing the dishes without being asked* • *Your children cleaning up their rooms on their own* • *A driver letting you change lanes in front of them* • *Someone letting you in line at the grocery store when they see you are in a hurry* • *A coworker helping you with copies*	Describe a recent example when your husband acted kindly toward you.
To make a lifetime habit of being kind, intentionally reach out to others daily through: • *a note* • *a phone call* • *a smile* • *a greeting* • *an e-mail* • *a thank you* • *a gift* • *a meal* • *initiating contact with your neighbors* • *helping a young mom* • *spending time with the elderly* • *speaking kindly to a store clerk*	In what ways have you shown kindness to your husband this week? How can you continue your kindness to him next week?
Don't just think about it, do it!	

Kindness is also a fruit of the Spirit living in us.

> *But the fruit of the Spirit is love, joy, peace, patience, kindness, goodness, faithfulness, gentleness, self-control…If we live by the Spirit, let us also walk by the Spirit. (Galatians 5:22-25)*

As we learn to walk in the Spirit, we will grow in kindness. We must continually ask God to help us with this attribute because it is His will for us to be kind. He will guide in deeds of kindness.

- Have you ever sensed the Spirit prompting you to reach out to someone?

- If so, and you did it, was there a sacrifice involved?

- In what ways did you learn to trust God?

Sometimes, when we feel happy or generous, we find it easy to be kind. Other times, when we are discouraged, hassled, or tired, we can scarcely summon the energy to utter a kind word. But God's commandment is clear. He intends that we make the conscious choice to treat others with kindness and respect, no matter our circumstances or emotions.

- What are some other attitudes, emotions, or circumstances that hinder kindness?

Words and kindness go hand in hand.

> *The tongue has the power of life and death, and those who love it will eat its fruit. (Proverbs 18:21 NIV)*

> *For the mouth speaks out of that which fills the heart. (Matthew 12:34)*

- Describe a time when words either blessed or ruined your day.

The way we approach a situation and react is in direct correlation to our relationship with the Lord. When we spend time with God, both in prayer and reading His Word, it can make an incredible difference in our lives.

> *So, as those who have been chosen of God, holy and beloved, put on a heart of compassion, kindness, humility, gentleness and patience; bearing with one another, and forgiving each other, whoever has a complaint against anyone; just as the Lord forgave you, so also should you. Beyond all these things put on love, which is the perfect bond of unity. Let the peace of Christ rule in your hearts, to which indeed you were called in one body; and be thankful. Let the word of Christ richly dwell within you, with all wisdom teaching and admonishing one another with psalms and hymns and spiritual songs, singing with thankfulness in your hearts to God. Whatever you do in word or deed, do all in the name of the Lord Jesus, giving thanks through Him to God the Father. (Colossians 3:12-17)*

Some practical suggestions for learning to speak kind words include:

- *Be aware of the importance of words.*
- *Pay attention to your words and consider when and how to use them wisely.*
- *Evaluate how your expressions may be perceived. Are your words disrespectful to your husband or harsh toward your children?*
- *Remember to value every person you meet.*
- *Regard every person as someone you can encourage in their relationship with Christ.*
- *Think and pray about your words before speaking.*

Can you think of an example of how your words drew someone closer to Jesus?

Can you think of a time when your words discouraged a friend or family member?

Think of specific ways you could show kindness to:

- A family member
- A church member
- A neighbor
- A coworker
- Your community
- A stranger

Other suggestions may include:

- Making a favorite food for your husband
- Giving your kids a break in their day with a special activity
- Calling or emailing your mother-in-law
- Thanking your pastor
- Making a meal for a new mom at church
- Inviting your neighbors to a BBQ
- Mowing an elderly neighbor's grass
- Helping someone at work catch up after a vacation
- Having a garage sale and giving the money to a charity
- Speaking respectfully to a waitress…and tipping well
- Buying lemonade from a child on a corner
- Giving a homeless person a small bag of groceries
- Filling a shoebox for *Operation Christmas Child*

What are other ideas or things you have done to show kindness?

Summary

Kindness is an intentional decision and action. Kindness may not come naturally, but it can be learned, practiced, and habitual. Kindness is also supernatural, it is a fruit of the Spirit. In *Love As a Way of Life*, Gary Chapman says, "Kindness means noticing someone else and recognizing his [or her] needs. It means seeing the value in every person we meet. And like every trait of a loving person, kindness can be much simpler, and more powerful, than we realize."[2]

Prayer

Lord Jesus, You are a perfect example of kindness and compassion to me. Thank You for forgiving me. Give me a compassionate heart full of kindness toward others. May people who observe me see my kindness to those I interact with daily. Amen.

Notes

---

[1] James Dobson, *Bringing Up Girls* (Carol Stream, IL: Tyndale House Publishers, Inc., 2010), p. 209.

[2] Gary Chapman, *Love as a Way of Life* (New York, NY: Doubleday, 2008), p. 16.

WOMANOFGRACE

An excellent wife, who can find? The heart of her husband trusts in her.

Christ Calls Us to Love Our Husbands

Older women…encourage the young women to love their husbands…so that the word of God will not be dishonored. (Titus 2:3-5)

Practicing grace by discovering practical ways to show love to our husbands.

Introduction

Paul's instruction to older women tasks them with a huge responsibility toward the young wives in the church. The salvation of others and the glory of God are at stake. The last thing we want is for God's name to be spoken against because of our behavior.

Can you think of an older couple who has been married for 40 or 50 years whose eyes still twinkle when they are together? Perhaps it would be easier to identify couples who have lived together for decades and seem miserable. It has been said that your imperfections are magnified as you get older. If that is true, we need to figure out *now* how to love our husbands well so that we become contented senior citizens. Jesus taught His disciples the principle of sowing and reaping (see Galatians 6:7). The reaping doesn't happen in the same season as the sowing. The farmer plants seeds in the spring but doesn't harvest his crop until the fall. We need to sow into our marriages now, so that we will be able to enjoy each other at our 50th anniversary parties.

God asks the Christian wife to love her husband (even if he is not a believer). She is to love him with all the energy and creativity she has. This will look different in each marriage. For a military wife, loving her husband may include getting up at "0-dark-thirty" to have coffee with him before he heads to the base. An older missionary friend realized that her husband wore a huge smile when she held his hand as they walked around Vienna. In Jan Karon's *Mitford* series, her leading lady brings joy to her husband (the stiff-collared Episcopal priest) by calling him "Dearest." For another woman, nothing makes her husband happier than when she frees up her day to spend it on the back of his motorcycle. The goal is to discover what will demonstrate love to your man and do it.

Biblical Foundation

> *Love is patient, love is kind. It does not envy, it does not boast, it is not proud. It is not rude, it is not self-seeking, it is not easily angered, it keeps no record of wrongs. Love does not delight in evil but rejoices with the truth. It always protects, always trusts, always hopes, always perseveres. Love never fails. But where there are prophecies, they will cease; where there are tongues, they will be stilled; where there is knowledge, it will pass away.* (1 Corinthians 13:4-8 NIV)

That is the truest test, isn't it? Can we make it until "death do us part" loving our husbands like *that*?

Choosing to Love

A teacher told her junior high class that they would have three major decisions to make in their lives.

- Whom will they serve?
- Whom will they marry?
- Who will raise their children?

If picking a mate is one of life's biggest decisions, why is it that some of us opt for somebody very different from ourselves? The honeymoon will be over pretty quickly. In a few months, you may realize you don't have that much in common after all. Experts suggest that we are attracted to our "opposite" because we strengthen and complete each other.

Think about the differences between you and your husband. (Often there's a night owl married to an early bird, a spender married to a penny-pincher, a messy married to a neatnik, or a confronter married to a peace-at-all-cost type).

- Were you aware of these differences before you married? How do you deal with them now?

Planning for your husband to change all of his character traits is not a good agenda. Love is giving up your wishes for the good of another. It means being content with the husband God gave you. It is not wishing he would be like your best friend's husband who does X, Y and Z for her. The grass is not greener on the other side of the fence. It may look that way, but it's only the chemicals they put on the lawn.

We are in a battle with Satan. The tempter plants discontentment in our minds. A Christian couple who loves each other and wants to honor God in their marriage sticks out like a sore thumb in our society. Satan does not want God to get that attention, so he is fighting hard to destroy Christian marriages.

Read Ephesians 6:10-14.

- Which two-word phrase is the key to resisting the devil's schemes?

- How can we do this in our marriages? Give some practical ways you can implement this strategy.

- James 4:7 also uses another strong verb to help in our battle with the devil. What is it?

- God knows this is a battle. In your marriage, you must take a stand against the enemy. Which practices will strengthen you?

If we are truly God's children, we are not alone. The Holy Spirit empowers us to love both passionately and sacrificially. Living that way pleases God and is a testimony to the world around us.

Five Ways to Love Your Husband

The topic of love is vast and worthy of our lifelong study. There are thousands of little and big things we may do to show love to our husbands, but here are a few ideas to get us started.

1. **Scrap your plan for his makeover.**

   Don't try to change him. Makeovers are God's business. Most often, when *we* try to change our husbands, it backfires and makes us both miserable.

   God asks us to love others as He loved us (1 John 4:7-11). This is the same love (Gr. *agape*) found in John 3:16, "For God so loved the world, that He gave His only begotten Son, that whoever believes in Him shall not perish, but have eternal life." That is how God loves, seeing something infinitely precious in the recipient of His love. He is self-sacrificing.

   In Philippians 2:5-8, we read again of Jesus' *agape* love. This One who is God became a man and humbled Himself even to the point of death on the cross. There is no greater love.

   - According to 1 Peter 3:1-2, when our husbands are disobedient to the Word, what may cause them to change?

   - Philippians 4:6 suggests another way to see change in our husbands. What is it?

   - Specifically what prayers would you offer to God for your husband?

Be ready to be changed yourself when you start to do these things. God refines us and smoothes our rough spots when we leave the changing work to Him.

2. **Recognize that your husband wants you to be his best friend.**

We began this chapter with Titus 2:4 which contains a Greek word for *love* that is not *agape* but *philandros*. It's from two words meaning to have affection for a dear friend who is a man.

This kind of affection is expressed in the very first human words recorded in Scripture:

> The LORD God said, "It is not good for the man to be alone. I will make a helper suitable for him."… So the LORD God caused the man to fall into a deep sleep; and while he was sleeping, he took one of the man's ribs and closed up the place with flesh. Then the LORD God made a woman from the rib he had taken out of the man, and he brought her to the man. The man said, "This is now bone of my bones, and flesh of my flesh; she shall be called 'woman,' for she was taken out of man." (Genesis 2:18, 21-23 NIV)

God gave Adam a friend and companion, someone who would join him in his life's work. That is the divine job description for a wife: to be a helper, or assistant, to her husband. We are called to help him be more productive and efficient at whatever God calls him to do. This may include his 9-to-5 job as well as your home life.

In decades past, when women were not typically employed outside the home, helping meant doing his laundry, having his coworkers and boss over for dinner, and being responsible for the care of the children and the home. Many women today are working outside the home. Both spouses must then juggle careers, family, and household responsibilities. Yet even in this situation, a wife's primary responsibility is to be a friend and helper to her husband.

- Do you enjoy being a companion and friend to your husband?

- What activities do you enjoy together?

- What do you do to help your husband? What attitude do you display in those times?

Peter gives us an example of *phileo* love:

> *To sum up, all of you be harmonious, sympathetic, brotherly, kindhearted, and humble in spirit; not returning evil for evil or insult for insult, but giving a blessing instead; for you were called for the very purpose that you might inherit a blessing. (1 Peter 3:8-9)*

We may at times forget to treat our husband as our best friend.

- Look at the words in the previous verse and consider how we are to live with one another.

- How can you become your husband's best friend?

Ideas to encourage friendship:

A. Find things you enjoy doing together. Begin cultivating them now so that when the children are gone you will have many common interests. A husband enjoys having his wife's company. It may not matter what the activity is, he just wants you with him.

- What activities did you do together when you were dating? Do you still enjoy those things?

- What could you learn to do that would thrill him?

B. Be his encourager and cheerleader. Friends build each other up. They notice the good and ignore the bad. Praise him in front of others, especially your children.

- When was the last time you praised him or told him you were proud of him?

C. Carry his burdens, even when it's a broken alternator. His hardest days may be when the car is in the shop or when there is stress at work.

- What hard thing is he going through right now? If you don't know, find out.

D. Get to know him.

- *Really* get to know him - what he likes and dislikes. What happy memories does he have from his childhood? What are his fears about the future? What are his hopes and dreams for the future?

- Pick one thing that would bless him and do it.

- Ask him what he'd like to do on his day off. Get a babysitter if you need to and just hang out with him. Let him decide everything that day - activities, food, etc.

3. **Lock the door and turn on the fan.**

   For this reason a man shall leave his father and mother and shall be joined to his wife, and the two shall become one flesh. (Ephesians 5:31)

This is *Song of Solomon*, "passionate lover" kind of love, not "buddy-buddy" love.

Understand that just as women need to talk it out or even share a good cry with their husbands to feel that emotional connection, husbands feel love most intensely through sexual intimacy. As one popular Christian teacher has said, "If you want to show your husband you love him, just show up naked."

Sex is one of the most important things we can do to demonstrate love to our husbands. According to Barbara Mouser in *Five Aspects of Woman*, there are only two areas or "worlds" where a man's masculinity can be affirmed - at work and in the bedroom. We can't do anything about the workplace, but we can refresh and bless him at home.

> *Drink water from your own cistern, running water from your own well. Should your springs overflow in the streets, your streams of water in the public squares? Let them be yours alone, never to be shared with strangers. May your fountain be blessed, and may you rejoice in the wife of your youth. A loving doe, a graceful deer—may her breasts satisfy you always, may you ever be captivated by her love. (Proverbs 5:15-19 NIV)*

God's design is that a wife will keep satisfying her husband for life. As author Gary Thomas explains in *Sacred Influence*:

> *[God] has called your husband to a holy lifestyle, and he zealously desires the growth of your husband's integrity.*

> *Anything [a wife] denies her husband becomes, by definition, an absolute denial, because he has no other place to which he can go to find satisfaction in a healthy or holy manner.*

> *Take a moment to ponder God's passionate love for the man you married. If only you could see how God and the angels celebrated on the day your husband became a believer, a redeemed servant of God's kingdom! If you could have glimpsed just three minutes of the rejoicing that erupted in heaven over this seemingly normal man whom not one person out of a hundred would describe as anything other than ordinary! You might just begin to realize how your attitude toward your husband's sexual needs and desires is, in fact, a matter of cosmic concern. On the day your husband became a believer, he accepted God's plan, not just for his eternity, but also for his sexuality. The world mocks that plan— one woman for life. No mental undressing of a celebrity or coworker. Not even an occasional leer at a barely dressed woman. No pornography. God calls him to an exclusive integrity that much of his society calls puritanical, fanatical, and flat-out unrealistic.*

> *Then God watches. Will this man have to live out God's call to purity without any real help from his wife? Will she participate reluctantly, grudgingly—motivated only by guilt—or with generosity, enthusiasm, and creativity?*

> *[…] a mutually satisfying sex life does wonderful things for a marriage. It knits a man's heart to his wife. It helps to protect his sexual integrity and keeps him from sinning against his God. It motivates him to please his wife, and it cements his loyalty to his home.[1]*

This joining and one-flesh love deepens the emotional connection (which is what wives want) and satisfies his sexual drive (which keeps husbands happy). There is an additional blessing which we learn about in Genesis 24:67: "Then Isaac brought her into his mother Sarah's tent, and he took Rebekah, and she became his wife, and he loved her; thus Isaac was comforted after his mother's death."

The Hebrew word for *comforted* means "to sigh" or "be consoled." How was Isaac comforted in his grief? Have you ever thought about sexual intimacy bringing healing and comfort?

4. **Keep the "joy, joy, joy, joy down in your heart."**

Don't depend on your husband to make you happy. Don't buy into the world's lie that says if you just find your soul mate, you will live happily ever after. Only God's love will ultimately satisfy you.

- What do we learn about God's love in Zephaniah 3:17 and Ephesians 3:16-19?

God did not make your husband to meet all your needs. He cannot, even if he tries. The only person who can meet your need for love is your Savior. He is the One who is unswervingly loyal to you. He is your ultimate Beloved because He loves perfectly.

In her article "A Life Worthy of the Calling," Autumn Ellis Ross states:

For nearly six decades, the Grahams have made their home in western North Carolina in a beautiful, yet humble, log cabin situated at the top of a mountain. Here Ruth lived like a single mother for most of her life…

A slightly-built woman, Ruth was nevertheless confident and very much her own person. Her strength and fierce passion for the Lord and her spirit of independence—unusual for her era—enabled her to do things that seemed impossible…

Ruth forged her own way, running her household and single-handedly raising five children the majority of their marriage. She modeled an independence from, yet unwavering support for, her husband. And when he returned home, she would always respectfully step aside. Allowing him to come back into the family system was a delicate dance requiring patience and submission to not only her husband, but also the Lord.

Ruth was the epitome of a woman whose own calling was to be a life partner in her husband's work.

[At the public funeral service for her mother, Ruth Bell Graham], Ruth Graham said of her, "My mother's happiness and fulfillment did not depend on circumstances. She was the lovely, beautiful, wise woman she was because early in her life she chose Christ as her center, her home, her purpose, her partner, her confidante, her example, and her vision."[2]

Ruth Graham did not depend upon her husband for her happiness. She had a deep joy that came from her relationship with Christ.

- Who is your confidante?

Another pastor's wife, Jill Briscoe, wrote, "Years ago I stopped looking to anyone but God to satisfy me." Her husband, Stuart, left for a three-month preaching trip without returning home, when she wrote this:

There is no man that can love me enough,
No child that can need me enough,
No job that can pay me enough, and
No experience that can satisfy me enough. Only Jesus.[3]

When we make God our first priority, and our Best Friend, we have an eternal source of joy. Our happiness comes from a strong, close bond with our Savior, Jesus Christ. There will probably be times when your life and marriage will get hard and you will encounter some very rough seas. Remember to take your burdens to the Lord. God will either quiet the storm or help you get through the stormy weather.

- Do you have a special place where you spend quiet time with God?

- How do you commune with Him?

What does all this have to do with loving our husbands? When we rely on God to satisfy our needs, we free our husbands from carrying a huge burden they were never designed to carry. You are not to be entirely dependent upon him to meet your emotional needs. Instead, take your concerns and fears to your loving heavenly Father who loves you perfectly.

5. Be the real deal.

Nothing proves the authenticity of our Christianity more than our marriages. Our husbands are carefully observing us. Our children are, also. Our neighbors are watching. We are silently preaching to them as they examine us. Nonbelievers won't take notice when we are just like the world—preoccupied with our appearance, body, income, houses, and standards of living. As

Christian women, we are to have an inner confidence and tranquility which comes from knowing who we are and whom we serve. We are exhorted to be excellent wives.

> *An excellent wife, who can find? For her worth is far above jewels. The heart of her husband trusts in her, and he will have no lack of gain. (Proverbs 31:10-11)*

An excellent wife is trustworthy. Her husband is strengthened in his role when he knows he has the trust of his wife. While our faith and character will be tested by trials, they are the very things Christ uses to authenticate our faith. Have we passed those tests consistently so that our husbands can predict how we will react? Trust means that both the facts and his feelings about us enable him to have confidence in us.

Putting it differently, can your husband fully trust you? Can he trust you with the credit card when you have the whole day to shop? Can he trust you at home to discipline the children even when you are worn out? Can he trust you to honor his parents? (See Ruth 3:11.) Can you handle emergencies in a Christ-like manner? Can he trust that you know what words to say (or not to say) when you talk with his coworkers or boss at a Christmas party? Can he rely on you when a handsome contractor comes to your home and he is not there?

Summary

Grace calls us to love our husbands well. The word *grace* lets us know that it is not always natural; it takes work. Yet God has designed us to be our husband's best friend and lover, so we must choose to love them this way. We will also bless them by being joyful, content, and trustworthy. By God's grace, we will become that kind of wife.

Prayer

Heavenly Father, thank you for our husbands. Make us godly wives of integrity who help our husbands in their God-given roles. Teach us how to love them with kind words, loving actions, and an understanding heart. Show us ways that we may encourage them as You guide them into the men You have designed them to be. Give them wisdom in their decisions. Keep them free from the temptations of this world. And help us, Lord, to love them unselfishly. Amen.

Notes
_____

[1] Gary Thomas, *Sacred Influence* (Grand Rapids, MI: Zondervan Publishing House, 2004), pp. 190-192, 203.

[2] Autumn Ellis Ross, "A Life Worthy of the Calling," *Wheaton College Alumni Magazine*, Fall 2007, pp. 26-28.

[3] Jill Briscoe, "Contentment or Corruption, Part Two, B," Alistair Begg's *Truth for Life* broadcast, August 11, 2010.

WOMANOFGRACE

> *Train up a child in the way he should go, even when he is old he will not depart from it.*

Christ Calls Us to Love Our Children

Behold, children are a gift of the Lord, the fruit of the womb is a reward. (Psalm 127:3)

Practicing grace by loving our children as we nurture, train, teach, and discipline them according to God's Word.

Introduction

To Christians, it seems logical that the apostle Paul would admonish us to love our children. But in Paul's day (first century A.D.), the culture of the Roman world was not "child friendly." John MacArthur comments, "Certain attitudes existed that made life perilous for children. For example, Rome had a law called *patria potestas*, which literally means 'the father's power.' The law allowed the father absolute control over every member of his family. He could sell them all as slaves; he could make them work in his fields in chains; he could even take the law into his own hands and punish any member of his family as severely as he wanted, including the imposition of the death penalty. And he had that power as long as he lived. Newborn children were customarily placed between the feet of the father, for example. If the father reached down and picked up the child, the child stayed in the home. But if the father turned and walked away, the child was literally thrown away." To further illustrate, MacArthur tells of a man writing to his wife and child in a letter dated 1 B.C. He wrote that he would send her his wages and "if —good luck to you —you have another child, if it is a boy, let it live: if it is a girl, throw it out."[1]

Biblical Foundation

God presents every one of our children to us as a gift. He specifically chooses each uniquely created child for us. He carefully places each child in his or her own specific home.

Think of Hannah, the childless Jewish woman in 1 Samuel 1. She was barren "because the Lord had closed her womb." When her family traveled to the temple to offer sacrifices, she was "greatly distressed, prayed to the Lord, and wept bitterly" because she was childless. We are also told that she called herself "oppressed in spirit" before pouring out her distressed soul before the Lord. The Lord answered her prayers and gave her a son, Samuel, whom she dedicated to the Lord even before he was born. Samuel went on to become a prophet in Israel.

- What does it mean to you to dedicate your child to the Lord?

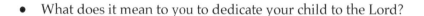

- What might be some of the implications of that decision that we might experience in our child's later life after we dedicate them to the Lord?

Behold, children are a gift of the Lord; the fruit of the womb is a reward. Like arrows in the hand of a warrior, so are the children of one's youth. How blessed is the man whose quiver is full of them. (Psalm 127:3-5a)

These verses tell us that children are a blessing from the Lord. He has given us the great responsibility and privilege of caring for and nurturing them in His ways, according to His instructions, for His purpose and plan for their lives.

Children are our *heritage*, defined as "that which comes from or belongs to one by birth." Our heritage does not consist of mere earthly possessions. It is the treasure of life experiences and wisdom that is passed down from one generation to another. You will pass the heritage of your life on to your children who will, in turn, pass it on to their children. The parenting we do today will affect not only our children, but also future generations.

- How do you think of your children as a heritage? What heritage are you passing on to your children?

- What do you want to be remembered for by your children and grandchildren?

You should prepare for the physical and spiritual welfare of your children in the unlikely event that both you and your husband die at the same time. This is not an easy subject to discuss, but it is wise to consider the possibility and plan accordingly. Who would you want to raise your children in your absence? Do you have family members whom you would want to take over their care? Have you made provision for this? Do you have a will? It is an important document in which your desires can be legally recorded. Everyone needs a will. If you die without one, the state has certain provisions that will take place unless you have specified differently. In a will, you can designate your wishes regarding guardians for your children. It does not have to be expensive. You can use resources found on the Internet and afterward have your document notarized by a notary public.

Things to consider when choosing guardians for your children:

1. Age and geographic location of the guardians in regard to other family members.

2. Their spiritual qualifications. (Are they Christians? Do they attend church regularly? Would they teach Christian truths to your children?)

3. Their philosophy of discipline and childrearing. (Do they have the same general standards of behavior that you do? Are they doing a good job of raising the children that they have now?)

4. Do they love children? Would they love raising yours?

5. Would they be willing and able to open up their home and heart to your children?

- Are there actions that you need to take? If so, what are they?

When you and your husband have selected potential guardians, ask if they are willing to take on this responsibility, should the need arise. Many people would feel privileged that you would consider them worthy to raise your children. After you have their consent, finalize the process and get it in writing.

Demonstrating Love Through Nurture and Training

For You formed my inward parts; You wove me in my mother's womb. I will give thanks to You, for I am fearfully and wonderfully made; wonderful are your works. (Psalm 139:13-14)

The beginning of the process of nurturing your children begins in your heart even before they are born, with attitudes, hopes, and dreams you have for them. In infancy, you demonstrate love by providing the necessities of life (food, clothing, warmth, cleanliness, love, and tenderness). As they grow, love will include training, teaching, and discipline.

Train up a child in the way he should go, even when he is old he will not depart from it. (Proverbs 22:6)

In studying the Proverbs, we must remember that they provide wise sayings and timely guidelines for living, rather than absolute promises for the future. With that in mind, we make an important observation about the previous verse: Each child needs to be trained in a distinct way, according to his own individual needs. His needs will be different from those of his siblings and friends. We need to be sensitive to our children and know them well enough that we are able to shape our training to fit each unique personality and need. We must be careful not to compare siblings to each other or to play favorites.

- How would you design a child-training plan for each of your children?

- What things would you consider?

Demonstrating Love Through Teaching

In Judges 13, we read the story of Manoah, the father of Samson. When it was revealed that Samson would deliver Israel from the hands of the Philistines as the future judge of Israel, Manoah's immediate response was to pray. He asked the Lord to send a man of God to "teach us what to do for the boy who is to be born." He realized that he needed help, and God provided. Today we are privileged to have God's Word which gives instruction as we raise our children. God's wisdom far exceeds that of any human resource. He will direct us through years of parenting and encourage us in the spiritual training of our children.

The apostle Paul instructed fathers to "bring [their children] up in the discipline and instruction of the Lord" (Ephesians 6:4). This shows that parents are responsible for the spiritual teaching of their children. Note that this duty has not been designated to the church, the pastor, the Sunday school teacher, the youth leader, or the Christian school. That does not mean that sources outside the family cannot be used to reinforce their teaching, but parents are to be the primary teachers for their children.

There are many ways that we teach our children, the first being our example. There is an old saying, "Actions speak louder than words." What we say to them will have little influence unless our behavior reinforces our words. God's Word gives us insight into the parents' responsibility for both the informal and formal teaching and training of our children.

Love the LORD your God with all your heart and with all your soul and with all your strength. These commandments that I give you today are to be upon your hearts. Impress them on your children. Talk about them when you sit at home and when you walk along the road, when you lie down and when you get up. (Deuteronomy 6:5-7 NIV)

The Jews were instructed to teach both the Word of God and the love of God to their children. They were to teach with diligence, having a purpose and a plan. They were to take everyday opportunities teaching them, "when you sit at home and when you walk along the road, when you lie down and when you get up." Basically, they were told to teach *all the time*. This is a good example for Christian parents as well.

Take advantage of the informal settings in daily life. Look for teachable moments to share the Word of God and spiritual truths with your children. Here are some ideas that may help you:

1. Observe God's creation as you take a walk, play outside, or look at the nighttime stars. Teach them God's power in creating the universe.

2. Pray with your child each day. Thank God for the food He provides. Ask Him to heal a sick relative or friend. Ask Him to provide for the needs of others. Pray for the salvation of an acquaintance or relative. When God answers your prayers, make it a point to thank Him in the presence of your child for His provision and faithfulness.

3. Teach your child to be the "hands and feet of Jesus" in your neighborhood. For example, take a meal to a sick friend, rake leaves for an elderly neighbor, or take cookies to a new neighbor.

4. Teach your child to give generously to the Lord. Encourage him to give an offering in church or Sunday school. As he gets older, he may earn his own money for a special project to support a missionary or a needy child. Teach and model sacrificial giving. One Christian family I know scaled down their usual Christmas gifts for the family and bought a goat for a needy family overseas. Christmas is a great time to teach your children to be givers. Consider giving special gifts to missionaries or collecting toys for a community toy drive. Fill shoeboxes for *Operation Christmas Child* or "adopt" a needy family or a lonely neighbor.

5. Minister together in your church or community. Take them with you when you serve in the nursery or children's church. Let them help in any way they are able. Volunteer to help with repairs around the church or cleaning. Visit the residents in a nursing home or hospital. Participate in community outreach events. Collect food for the needy. Serve in a soup kitchen.

   - What is the Holy Spirit prompting you to do?

Formal teaching takes place when we intentionally sit down with our children, open the Word of God, and teach them principles for godly living. It's never too early to begin. Even toddlers can learn to pray, sing songs to Jesus, and memorize a simple verse. For example, on Ann Voskamp's blog, *A Holy Experience*, she shares that at each mealtime they eat bread and take in the Bread of Life. Their Bibles are kept in buckets at the table. During each meal, they read a few verses and discuss them. Remember that all your teaching should be age-appropriate, considering the length of your child's attention span and ability to sit still.

Suggestions on how to begin:
- Start with reading a Bible story and discussing how it applies to your child's life.
- Teach your child to pray his own simple prayers.
- Sing songs together with lots of motions or learn to sign the words in ASL.
- Act out Bible stories by making them into exciting skits.
- Have them draw a picture or make a collage or diorama of a Bible story you are studying.
- Memorize Scripture together.
- As children get older, study a book of the Bible and discuss short passages.
- When your children are capable, teach them to have their own personal devotions. Provide them with an age-appropriate Bible and the tools they need such as a reference book, journal, or study guide.
- Pray with and for your children, in their presence.

- Make a list of prayer requests for each member of the family. Include unsaved family members and friends.

- Pray for missionaries, especially those that your children know personally.

- Present the way of salvation to your children.

Besides formal Bible teaching, there are many ways to encourage the faith of our children. You may read Christian novels such as *The Pilgrim's Progress* by John Bunyan or *The Chronicles of Narnia* by C. S. Lewis. Read books about Christian missionaries or great heroes of the faith and talk about their contribution to the world. For a family fun night, watch a *VeggieTales* video together and enjoy a treat. Discuss the moral of the story and how it applies to their life. Take a special vacation or field trip to a place that features the truth of God's creation such as a planetarium, aquarium, or zoo. The goal of your instruction is to make the Word of God come alive. The more you vary the content and format, the more they will look forward to this time together as a family.

- Have you and your husband discussed a plan for family devotions?

- List some ways that you can begin to instill God's Word in the lives of your children.

Demonstrating Love Through Discipline

Definitions of discipline include: 1) to instruct or educate, to inform the mind, to prepare by instructing in correct principles and habits; 2) to correct, to chastise, to punish. Most people focus only on the punitive aspect of discipline. The Bible supports loving discipline because God disciplines His children whom He loves.

> *For those whom the Lord loves He disciplines, and He scourges every son whom He receives. It is for discipline that you endure; God deals with you as with sons; for what son is there whom his father does not discipline? (Hebrews 12:6-7)*

Discipline can be divided into two main categories—*preventive* and *corrective*. Preventive discipline can also be called "training in righteousness." It includes all your instructions that will result in Christlikeness in your child. Corrective discipline is punishment for disobedience. Both are needed to properly train and teach our children scriptural principles.

Why is discipline necessary for our children? These verses help answer the question:

- *For all have sinned and fall short of the glory of God. (Romans 3:23)*

- *Foolishness is bound up in the heart of a child; the rod of discipline will remove it far from him. (Proverbs 22:15)*

- *Do not withhold discipline from a child; if you punish him with the rod, he will not die. Punish him with the rod and save his soul from death. (Proverbs 23:13 NIV)*

First, we need to discipline our children so they learn there is a greater authority outside themselves. Also, children need discipline to protect them from a world they are not mature enough to handle. We must ask the Lord for wisdom and guidance in discerning how to carry out this task.

The first thing we must note is the rebellious spirit of our young children. The point of discipline is to shape their spirit in obedience to authority. At every stage of our child's life, we must evaluate how to address this. It is important that you and your husband agree on what form of discipline will achieve this goal for each child. As we teach and train our children toward this goal, we are practicing preventive discipline.

- What are the ways each of your children display a rebellious spirit?

- What plans and rules have you and your husband established concerning discipline?

Children, be obedient to your parents in all things, for this is well-pleasing to the Lord. (Colossians 3:20)

Use God's Word to instruct your child in obedience. This is part of preventive discipline. This discipline is just as important as corrective punishment. It takes place before and after corrective punishment. For instance, we tell him, "Do not play in the street." We explain to him the dangers involved, that we expect his obedience, and that we will punish him if he disobeys. After the child plays in the street, we take him aside and punish him appropriately. This is corrective in nature. Then we tell him how much we love him and are concerned with his safety. We hug him, and again tell him the dangers involved.

Corrective discipline is often difficult for both parents and their children. Methods of punishment are numerous. They may include: discussion, time-out, withholding privileges, taking away toys, grounding, or whatever method shapes your child's temperament the best. All discipline must be age-appropriate. There are excellent resources written on the subject. Take time to read and discuss them with your husband. Strive to come to an agreement.

The most important rule for parents in disciplining their children is consistency. That means that you must correct your child *every* time he disobeys, and then punish him appropriately. Inconsistency exasperates the rebellious spirit. He feels insecure and will begin to ignore your rules because he doubts whether he will be punished. Children need boundaries. Boundaries provide security. Without boundaries a child becomes frustrated and will "test for boundaries." This causes more disobedience. Our failure to discipline may cause our children to sin.

Another important thing to remember is not to make threats unless you plan to carry them out. Be careful with your words. Think twice before using these two words—*never* and *always*. If you fail to follow through with your threats even once, your correction will be ineffective because the child will soon realize that you don't intend to deliver the consequences you promised.

Specific times when children *need* discipline:

- When a child breaks a rule

- When his safety is involved

- When he hurts others or their property

- When he wants his own way and refuses to obey the authority over him

There are times when correction is necessary but punishment is not. Alway make sure that he understands why he is being corrected.

One of the most important things that you will teach your children is obedience. The apostle Paul gives instructions to children in these verses concerning obedience:

> *Children, obey your parents in the Lord, for this is right. Honor your father and mother (which is the first commandment with a promise), so that it may be well with you, and that you may live long on the earth. (Ephesians 6:1-3)*

Obedience is necessary if we are to enjoy happy, God-honoring lives within our families. If our children first learn to obey their parents, they will later learn to obey teachers, policemen, and others that exercise authority over them. Learning transfers. Once it is learned well in one situation, it can be put into practice in other venues. If we never learn to obey our parents (whom we see), we probably won't learn to obey God (whom we don't see).

A French diplomat once asked George Washington's mother what she believed to be the most important thing she had taught her son. Without hesitation she replied, "I taught him to obey."

God desires obedience from His children. Obedience is an outward sign of an inward attitude and conviction that God's will is best for our life and that we are conforming to His plan for us.

All discipline for the moment seems not to be joyful, but sorrowful; yet to those who have been trained by it, afterwards it yields the peaceful fruit of righteousness. (Hebrews 12:11)

The writer of Hebrews instructs us that discipline is often sorrowful. Punishment must produce sorrow and repentance if it is to be effective. The reward of effective discipline is behavior that demonstrates righteousness. Our motivation for discipline is a deep desire to obey God and to raise our children in the nurture and admonition of the Lord. We want them to obey out of love for the Lord and their parents, not just fear of punishment. Remember to discipline in love, not anger.

- What are the expectations in your home regarding your child's behavior? Are they clear?

- How often do you reevaluate them?

Demonstrating Love Through Instilling Character Qualities

Ephesians 5:1 tells us to be imitators of God. We want our children to imitate Him, too. What character qualities and principles should we attempt to instill in them? Some suggestions might be:

- Love and respect for God and parents
- Giving to God and others
- Honesty
- Forgiveness
- Self-control
- How to deal with temptations

Ask God to help you decide which virtues you need to work on first. As children get older, teach them responsibility, independence, decision-making, problem solving, goal setting, and handling money wisely. All of these skills are necessary as your child moves into adulthood. Remember that all the teaching and training you do as parents is in preparation for the day when your child will leave home and begin to function responsibly in the world around him.

Cherish each day with your children. Relax and enjoy them because it's only the "blink of an eye" between kindergarten, high school graduation, and wedding gowns. Pray that when this takes place, your child will have learned the importance of loving, honoring, and serving Jesus Christ.

- What are some character traits that you would like to begin instilling in your children?

- How does your behavior reflect and promote these traits?

More Helpful Parenting Tips

- Make your child feel special. Remember to make memories, even on ordinary days. Develop holiday traditions for your family that are yours alone. Make birthdays occasions to remember.

- Teach good manners to your children. It will help them relate to others with confidence. Begin at an early age. Manners should become a part of your child's conduct for a lifetime. Find outside sources if you need help in this area.

- Use Scripture as a springboard to pray for your children. (Example: *Father, I pray that [my child] will reject the way of a fool that is right in his own eyes, and that he/she will be wise and listen to counsel. Proverbs 12:15*)

- Study to discover each child's love language. Encourage and bless them accordingly.

- Write love notes and share special thoughts by putting them in your child's lunches, camp suitcases, or under pillows.

- Choose personalized gifts for special occasions or when you are going on a trip. (Example: For your artist, choose a new set of paints and a canvas. For your baseball player, buy a new batting glove or some baseball cards.)

- Spend one-on-one time with each of your children by taking them on a special excursion to a place they enjoy.

- Plan a special getaway or event together to mark an important milestone in their life. I know one mom who took each of her daughters away for their thirteenth birthday.

- Begin reading to your child at an early age when they can still cuddle up in your lap. If you want your children to love reading, begin while they are toddlers.

- Value your child's worth. Look for ways to let them know you love them for who they are—the way God made them. Don't make your love dependent on things they have done like getting all A's on a report card or hitting a home run in the baseball game.

- Give each child special tasks to perform in the home. Match a child's interests, abilities, and talents to family responsibilities and chores. (*The Treasure Tree* by John Trent & Gary Smalley and *The Two Trails* by John Trent provide helpful lists.)

Encouragement for Moms

It has been said that "being a mom is the hardest job that you will ever love!" Motherhood is an awesome but exhausting experience. It is easy at times to feel both isolated and overwhelmed, especially while your children are very young. You are not in this alone. Your husband should also be actively involved in your child's upbringing. The Lord gave parental roles to both of you. He is capable of helping.

- Discuss the child-rearing process with your husband. Ask him how he plans to participate. How will you seek to include him?

It is important to remember that your relationship with your husband is more important than your relationship with your children. Marriage is a long-term goal. Parenting is a short-term goal. Your parenting responsibilities usually last about twenty years. Marriage is *till death do us part*.

Tips for Moms

The Lord also gives us other relationships so that this time need not be lonely. Develop some good friendships. Women friends can encourage us in special ways that husbands would not consider doing. Friendships do not always happen spontaneously, so be proactive in cultivating them. Ask God to help in this process. Pray for a wise Christian woman to come into your life. Ask one to mentor you or be your prayer partner. Try trading babysitting time with other mothers. Form a play group with other moms that have children the same ages as your children.

Summary

Persevere in the task that God has given you. Your labor of love will someday be rewarded with the knowledge that you have devoted your life to training your children in the ways of the Lord, trusting Him to do His good work in their lives.

Prayer

Lord, thank You for the gift of children. I thank You for entrusting us as parents with their care, nurture, love, teaching, and discipline. Thank You for giving us Your guidance and wisdom in Your Word. Help us to apply that direction and guidance as we seek to raise our children to glorify You. Be with us as we entrust them to Your plan for their life. Amen.

Note

[1] John MacArthur, *The Family* (Chicago, IL: Moody Press, 1982), pp. 98-99.

WOMAN OF GRACE

Watch over your heart with all diligence, for from it flow the springs of life.

Christ Calls Us to Purity

Therefore if you have been raised up with Christ, keep seeking the things above, where Christ is, seated at the right hand of God. Set your mind on the things above, not on the things that are on earth. (Colossians 3:1-2)

Practicing grace by remaining pure in every aspect of our lives—thoughts, speech, actions, and sex.

Introduction

Purity means clean, free from physical or moral pollution, innocent, chaste, not contaminated. A spiritual definition is *the moral excellence I demonstrate in my life as I consistently do what is right.*

The Greek word *hagnos* means fleeing from ceremonial defilement, holy, sacred, chaste, free from sin, innocent.

Our worldly culture is "embarrassing the angels," cries Peggy Noonan, a columnist for

The Wall Street Journal.[1] Dr. James Dobson, in *Bringing Up Girls,* warns that "If MTV, Hollywood, the pop music industry, and peers have their way with your girls, they are likely to curse, dress provocatively, behave like uncultured and uncouth waifs, and have no sense of personal dignity. Remember, Mom, you are the keeper of the keys at home."[2] Under the world's influences, our daughters will learn to despise their bodies, experiment sexually, and view marriage as an outdated institution.

It is our job as wives and mothers to set the standard, to be the model and teacher of sexual purity and moral excellence. This is a tall order indeed in such a confused and sinful world, yet the reward is abundant life now and for eternity: "Blessed are the pure in heart, for they shall see God" (Matthew 5:8).

Carolyn Mahaney, author of *Feminine Appeal* says, "If you watch TV, go to the movies, or read magazines today, you can get the idea that the only people having sex (or "good sex") are the ones who aren't married. If marital sex is even portrayed in popular media, it seems bland or routine. Our culture has pushed marital sex into the back room and instead *celebrates* immoral sex." She continues by stressing the need for older women to train younger women in a biblical perspective of sex: "Marital union and fidelity allow a husband and wife to wholly delight in each other, without the consequences and contamination that accompany sinful sex. Purity's pleasure is receiving sex as a wonderful gift from our Creator and enjoying it for His glory."[3]

Purity for a Christian begins with a clean heart. The first step is asking forgiveness from Jesus Christ who shed His blood to pay for our sins. Next is keeping current accounts with God—asking for forgiveness daily when we sin (1 John 1:9) and setting our minds on the things above where Christ dwells (Colossians 3:15). Finally, we need empowerment by the Holy Spirit to overcome immorality, impurity, passion, evil desire, greed, and idolatry (Galatians 5:19-21).

Biblical Foundation

[20] My son, give attention to my words; incline your ear to my sayings. [21] Do not let them depart from your sight; keep them in the midst of your heart. [22] For they are life to those who find them and health to all their body. [23] Watch over your heart with all diligence, for from it flow the springs of life. [24] Put away from you a deceitful mouth and put devious speech far from you. [25] Let your eyes look directly ahead and let your gaze be fixed straight in front of you. [26] Watch the path of your feet and all your ways will be established. [27] Do not turn to the right nor to the left; turn your foot from evil. (Proverbs 4:20-27)

Restate the instructions for guarding your heart in these verses:

- Proverbs 4:24

- Proverbs 4:25

- Proverbs 4:26-27

Protect your heart by guarding your mouth

Put away from you a deceitful mouth and put devious speech far from you. (Proverbs 4:24)

- What do you think it means to guard your mouth?

But no one can tame the tongue; it is a restless evil and full of deadly poison. (James 3:8)

- What does James 3:8 tell us about the tongue?

For the mouth speaks out of that which fills the heart. (Matthew 12:34b)

- What does Matthew 12:34b tell us?

- Can you give an example of how this has been true in your life?

Let the words of my mouth and the meditation of my heart be acceptable in Your sight, O Lord, my rock and my Redeemer. (Psalm 19:14)

- This is an important prayer. What do you think is acceptable speech to the Lord? Refer to the following verses:

Ephesians 4:2

Psalm 118:24

Luke 6:37

Galatians 6:2

Psalm 106:1

Psalm 37:7

Protect your heart by guarding your eyes

Let your eyes look directly ahead and let your gaze be fixed straight in front of you. (Proverbs 4:25)

- What do you think it means to guard your eyes?

What is the source of quarrels and conflicts among you? Is not the source your pleasures that wage war in your members? You lust and do not have; so you commit murder. You are envious and cannot obtain; so you fight and quarrel. (James 4:1-2)

Then He said to them, "Beware, and be on your guard against every form of greed; for not even when one has an abundance does his life consist of his possessions." (Luke 12:15)

I have made a covenant with my eyes; how then could I gaze at a virgin? (Job 31:1)

- How do these verses expand your thoughts on guarding your eyes?

Protect your heart by watching your steps

Watch the path of your feet and all your ways will be established. Do not turn to the right nor to the left; turn your foot from evil. (Proverbs 4:26-27)

- What do you think it means to watch your steps?

Consider how these verses alert you to precautions you can take to protect yourself.

He awakens Me morning by morning, He awakens My ear to listen as a disciple. (Isaiah 50:4b)

Your word is a lamp to my feet and a light to my path. (Psalm 119:105)

Do you not know that you are a temple of God and that the Spirit of God dwells in you? (1 Corinthians 3:16)

Then Jesus said to His disciples, "If anyone wishes to come after Me, he must deny himself, and take up his cross and follow Me." (Matthew 16:24)

We have only touched the surface of what it means to guard your heart. Other important aspects would include: knowing God's promises, being content, practicing gratitude, communing with God regularly, and living purposefully. Linda Dillow's *Calm My Anxious Heart* would be a great follow-up to this lesson.

Purity in Marriage

For this reason a man shall leave his father and his mother, and be joined to his wife; and they shall become one flesh. And the man and his wife were both naked and were not ashamed. (Genesis 2:24-25)

- Why does God consider sex to be a beautiful thing?

Carolyn Mahaney reminds us, "God made man and woman to be sexual creatures. God did not wince when Adam, in seeing Eve, was drawn to her sexually. God didn't cringe when Adam and Eve enjoyed sexual relations in the Garden of Eden. In His wise and perfect design, He gave sexual desire to both the man and the woman.

Our sexual desire is not evil because God Himself has created it. He is not embarrassed about our sexual nature, and neither should we be embarrassed."

She continues: "God gave sexual desire to both male and female; however, God imposed restrictions upon our sexual appetites. His Word prohibits sexual activity prior to marriage and mandates complete fidelity within marriage (1 Corinthians 7:1-9). These boundaries are for our good—so we can enjoy the sheer delight and reap the sweet rewards that flow from obedience to Him."[4]

Some of us are more comfortable than others when discussing sex. Depending on your age, background, and past experiences, this can be a difficult part to this lesson. Two books that may assist you in gaining a correct biblical perspective are Carolyn Mahaney's *Feminine Appeal* and Linda Dillow's *Intimate Issues*.

> *Marriage should be honored by all, and the marriage bed kept pure, for God will judge the adulterer and all the sexually immoral. (Hebrews 13:4 NIV)*

Not everyone comes into a marriage innocent and free from a sexual past. But God is faithful to forgive, to purify hearts, and to give new beginnings.

- How may we have a clean heart?

> *If a man cleanses himself…he will be an instrument for noble purposes, made holy, useful to the Master and prepared to do any good work. Flee the evil desires of youth, and pursue righteousness. (2 Timothy 2:21-22a NIV)*

- If we are to be sanctified, useful vessels to our Master (Christ), what are we to do when we experience evil desires?

> *Flee from sexual immorality. All other sins a man commits are outside his body, but he who sins sexually sins against his own body. Do you not know that your body is a temple of the Holy Spirit, who is in you, whom you have received from God? You are not your own; you were bought at a price. Therefore honor God with your body. (1 Corinthians 6:18-20 NIV)*

- What makes sexual purity so important to God?

Tying It All Together

No one gets married expecting the relationship to fail. As Betty Huizenga writes in *Apples of Gold*, "Seldom do people fall into serious sin because they planned to do it. More often it begins with an unhappy or angry heart looking for satisfaction or by a small argument that gets out of hand. This is especially true of infidelity. Before we can even think about it, we are lost in sins that envelop us and unravel our lives."[5]

1 Corinthians 10:12 warns us, "Therefore let him who thinks he stands take heed that he does not fall." Oddly, statistics show that two-thirds of divorces are initiated by women.

- Why do you think this is true?

- Are women tempted in the same way as men?

Life is never the fairy tale we imagined we would live. Real husbands and wives have lots of issues and lots of disappointments. If we continually live in selfishness, insisting on our own way with our spouse and God, we will fall into sin. Disappointment leads to unloving attitudes and discontentment. Harsh words lead to withdrawal, loss of sexual intimacy, and contemplated alternatives. Broken hearts result in words of divorce, anger, bitterness, and an inability to trust our spouse or God.

- How have you noticed this pattern in marriages?

- Have you ever seen this pattern stopped before the marriage failed? What did they do?

- What steps can you take to avoid this path?

- In what areas might you be vulnerable to falling into sin?

Summary

In the days when Jesus walked the earth, as a young woman reached the age of marriage, her family would purchase an alabaster box and fill it with precious ointment. The size of the box and the value of the ointment would parallel the family's wealth – it would be part of her dowry. When a young man came to ask for her hand, she would respond by breaking the alabaster box at his feet. This anointing not only showed him honor, but also expressed that she was surrendering her life to him, her hopes, dreams, and future.

One day, as Jesus was eating in the house of Simon the leper, a sexually immoral woman broke her alabaster box and poured the valuable ointment on Jesus' head (Luke 7, Mark 14). This was not an acceptance of a marriage proposal, it was a surrender of her life into the hands of the only One who could pardon her past sexual sin and secure her eternal destiny. When we surrender our lives and hopes into Jesus' care, He brings purity, peace, and hope for the future.

Prayer

Father and Savior, we bow before You and worship You alone. Thank You for calling us to Yourself as Your bride. Forgive us for choosing our own way instead of Yours. Help us to be faithful to honor You in our minds, hearts, and bodies. Give us the strength to speak and walk as You would desire. Teach us to be godly wives and mothers who demonstrate purity for Your honor and glory. In Jesus' precious name, Amen.

Notes

[1] Peggy Noonan, "Embarrassing the Angels," *The Wall Street Journal*, March 2, 2006.

[2] James Dobson, *Bringing Up Girls* (Carol Stream, IL: Tyndale House Publishers, Inc., 2010), p. 58.

[3] Carolyn Mahaney, *Feminine Appeal* (Wheaton, IL: Crossway, 2003), pp. 81-82.

[4] Carolyn Mahaney, *Feminine Appeal* (Wheaton, IL: Crossway, 2003), p. 83.

[5] Betty Huizenga, *Apples of Gold* (Colorado Springs, CO: Cook Communications, 2000), p. 90.

WOMANOFGRACE

*Wives, be
subject to
your own
husbands,
as to the
Lord.*

Christ Calls Us to Submit to Our Husbands

*For you were called to freedom, brethren; only do not
turn your freedom into an opportunity for the flesh,
but through love serve one another. (Galatians 5:13)*

Practicing grace by demonstrating
love for our husbands in graciously
acknowledging their headship and
following Christ's lead in humble
submission.

Introduction

When we submit to our husbands, we express
love for God and His Word. Every act, no
matter how menial, is a visible demonstration
of love. It's another way of living worthy of the
gospel. When we voluntarily serve, we reflect
the humility of Christ which is so contrary to
human nature. Christ wants authentic
followers, and submission proves our
commitment to Him. We become a kind of
missionary to a world eagerly longing for
healthy, God-honoring relationships.

Biblical Foundation

Wives, be subject to your own husbands, as to the Lord. For the husband is the head of the wife, as Christ also is the head of the church, He Himself being the Savior of the body. But as the church is subject to Christ, so also the wives ought to be to their husbands in everything…and the wife must see to it that she respects her husband. (Ephesians 5:22-24, 33b)

When we accept God's gracious gift of salvation, we are no longer strangers to Him. We become members of His family. We belong in His household with every other Christian. Our thoughts and attitudes adjust to fit our new situation.

Using inductive Bible study methods, let's glean information about godly submission by considering the questions - *Who? What? When? Why? and How?*

1. **To whom should we submit?**

    A. _____ James 4:7

    B. _____ Romans 13:1

    C. _____ Ephesians 5:22

The list isn't that long. (That's encouraging, isn't it?)

Who is the biblical example of submission in 1 Peter 3:1-6? _____ Read her story in Genesis 12:1-5.

In *God Speaks to Women Today*, author Eugenia Price imagines a conversation between Abraham and Sarah like this:

"I have something important to tell you…We're going to leave Ur, Sarai. God spoke to me, and told me to go…. As clearly as a man can hear, I heard the voice of the true God say to me: 'As for you, leave your land, your relatives and your father's household for a land which I will show you, and I will make you into a great nation.'…I do not understand it, Sarai, but He has spoken, and I cannot refuse to obey Him."

This time, perhaps the first time in their married lives, Abram was not asking her opinion. He was stating a fact. They were going. There seemed to be no choice. He was not brusque, merely strong with the strange, new certainty. With no argument, Sarai began making plans to break up her comfortable home. She saw that their portable belongings were packed, and piece by beloved piece, she watched her magnificent, hand-carved furniture being sold or given away. She sorted her linens, gave the perplexed servants endless orders, sent messages to friends explaining almost nothing, and watched familiar possessions disappear through the courtyard of her home.[1]

Sarah was not a young bride at this point, she was sixty-five years old, and her husband was ten years older. They had lived all their lives in this upscale, bustling city. Abraham's father was a leading idol maker. There was plenty of income. Sarah had expensive clothes, a beautiful two-storied home, servants, and everything she could want. Leaving her home was not easy. Her life was changing dramatically.

- How would you respond if your husband told you that there was a big change on the horizon?

- Has this happened to you? If so, how did you respond?

In *Her Name is Woman*, Gien Karssen writes: "Abraham had obeyed immediately. Sarah had adjusted to the decision.... Like Abraham, she had a strong personality with a well-developed character.... She definitely had a mind of her own, yet she had been able to give herself to him because of an inner freedom."[2] Sarah was willing to follow her husband as they traveled to the unknown. This submission was beautiful and precious to God, eventually resulting in a son, Isaac, the fulfillment of God's promise to Abraham.

2. **What is submission?**

The word *submission* comes from the Greek word *hupotasso* which literally means "to place under," "to arrange in an orderly fashion," or "to assign position."

From the Old Testament, we learn about submission from some very special women:

A. To whom did Ruth submit in Ruth 2:8? What was the outcome of her submission in Ruth 4:13 and Matthew 1:5?

B. To whom did Esther submit in Esther 2:10, 2:20, 4:8, and 4:14? What was the outcome of her submission?

From the New Testament, we learn about perfect submission:

   A. To whom did Jesus submit in Luke 2:51?

   B. To whom did Jesus submit in Luke 22:42?

Submission includes humbling oneself. Ruth first submitted to Naomi by going to a specific field to work. Then she submitted to Boaz, resulting in her placement in the line of Christ. Esther, a beautiful Jewish woman, listened to what her cousin, Mordecai, told her to do. Because she submitted to him, she saved the Jews from destruction. Jesus entrusted His life into the hand of His Father. Because of His submission, there is eternal life for all who believe.

3. **What submission is not.**

Submission is not about worth or value, inequality or inferiority. It's not about who is the better decision-maker. It does not mean that a wife should withhold her input or her influence from her husband. Neither does it imply that husbands are more spiritual or have a closer connection to God. Submission is not about becoming doormats. It does not mean that you should change your personality. It does not make you a robot, and it does not permit abuse.

In *Loving Your Husband*, Cynthia Heald shares Chuck Swindoll's cautions regarding difficult situations:

> *It is one thing to be in subjection. It is another thing entirely to become the brunt of indignity, physical assault, sexual perversion, and uncontrolled rage…At such crisis times, call for help! Seek out a Christian friend who can assist you. Talk with your pastor or a competent counselor who will provide both biblical guidance and emotional support. And pray! Pray that your Lord will bring about changes in the unbearable circumstances surrounding you. Ask for deliverance, safety, stability, and great grace to see you through, to settle your fears, to calm your spirit so you can think and act responsibly.*[3]

Elizabeth Elliott was a young missionary wife in Ecuador in the 1950s. Her husband was murdered by the tribe they went to evangelize, the Auca Indians. In *Let Me Be a Woman*, she wrote to her daughter who was about to be married, and said of submission, "It does not lead to self-destruction, the stifling of gifts, personhood, intelligence and spirit…God is not asking anybody to become a zero…With gladness [a wife] submits because she understands that voluntary submission is her very strength. Because it is the thing asked of her by her Creator…."[4]

What does Galatians 3:26-29 teach about women and men?

4. When do we submit?

Ephesians 5:24 gives us the answer: _____

Again, Sarah is our example. See Genesis 12:10-18 and 20:2-3. Sarah obeyed her husband when he told her to say she was his sister instead of his wife so he wouldn't be killed. Sarah did what her husband asked her to do, twice, and both times God protected her. God intervened and stopped Abraham's foolish plan. Sarah submitted to her husband's unwise decision, but God rescued her. God is always in ultimate control. There may, however, be a time when a wife's submission to God must take precedence over submission to her husband. It will be a rare instance that your husband will ask you to do something immoral. In this case, you must submit to God's authority and not sin.

The word "obey" is politically incorrect in today's world. In *Strike the Original Match*, Chuck Swindoll says, "Before your feathers get ruffled by what this says of Sarah ("obeyed"), it will help you to realize the Greek verb means 'to pay close attention to' someone. It's the idea of attending to the needs of another."[5] It means literally "to hear under." Sarah heard what her husband wanted and helpfully responded to him. She listened and followed the leader.

> *Husbands, love your wives, just as Christ also loved the church and gave Himself up for her, so that He might sanctify her, having cleansed her by the washing of water with the word, that He might present to Himself the church in all her glory, having no spot or wrinkle or any such thing; but that she would be holy and blameless...This mystery is great; but I am speaking with reference to Christ and the church. (Ephesians 5:25-27, 32)*

Marriage is a beautiful picture of the relationship Christ has with His beloved bride, the Church. When we realize that God has placed our husband's loving authority over us, we can submit to his leadership in our marriages. Our husbands are called to love sacrificially as we are called to submit.

> *[…] the relationship of Jesus to the church had been the model for that of a husband and wife. We, the church, submit to Christ in everything, and the parallel of a wife submitting "everything" to her husband is no longer daunting, since we know what kind of behavior the husband has been called on to imitate. To what role must he submit? To that of savior, a servant-leader, who uses his authority and power to express a love that doesn't even stop at dying for the beloved. (The Meaning of Marriage, Timothy Keller)[6]*

Jesus exemplifies submission. Within the marriage relationship the wife has the privilege of imitating His humility. While submission is not natural for us, it is something we will learn and do because we are Christ-followers.

5. Why should we submit?

Because the creation order calls for submission.

In their book *Recovering Biblical Manhood and Womanhood*, John Piper and Wayne Grudem, explain it this way: When the Bible teaches that men and women fulfill different roles in relation to each other, charging man with a unique leadership role, it bases this differentiation not on temporary cultural norms but on permanent facts of creation… In the Bible, differentiated roles for men and women are never traced back to the fall of man and woman into sin. Rather, the foundation of this differentiation is traced back to the way things were in Eden before sin warped our relationships. Differentiated roles were corrupted, not created, by the fall. They were created by God.[7]

The divine chain of command is clear from 1 Corinthians 11:1-3,11-12.

- To whom is the wife responsible?

- To whom is the husband responsible?

Our assigned roles are different. Men are given the responsibility of leading their families. Wives are given the privilege of being helpmates to their husbands. God made us to function together, just differently.

- How is this worked out in your family?

6. **How can we submit?**

A. It begins with respect.

Respect literally means "to fear." We naturally respect those in a position of authority, like policemen, the president, and IRS agents. We don't belittle their authority because it is connected to their job. This *fear* includes awe, honor, and high esteem. In Sarah's case, she called Abraham "lord" (not "Lord"). She used a respectful title like *sir* even though he wasn't her supreme Lord.

In *Love and Respect*, Dr. Emerson Eggerichs proposes the concept of the "crazy cycle"—she can't respect him because he doesn't love her well, but he can't love her well when he doesn't feel respected. It goes on and on until someone takes a first step in breaking the cycle.

It's easier for wives to submit to someone they respect and trust. Even if your husband has done many things wrong already, finding something to respect him for is a starting point. Start today to encourage him. Focus on his good qualities. What did you admire about him when you were dating?

- List qualities of your husband that are worthy of your respect and admiration:

B. Let the Holy Spirit control your attitude.

The Holy Spirit empowers us to please God. This doesn't come from trying harder. It comes from growing in His grace through reading, studying, and memorizing Scripture, fellowshipping with godly people, meditating on and listening to the still small voice of the Holy Spirit in prayer, and slowly maturing in your Christian life. A spiritually mature woman knows that by giving up control she models love and obedience to God in a tangible way because God said it very clearly—He wants the husband to lead the family.

Read Ephesians 5:18-21 and Galatians 5:22-23.

- Write one of your *natural* responses and compare it to a response controlled by the Holy Spirit.

- How does following the leading of the Holy Spirit enhance your marriage?

C. Put your hope in God.

A submissive wife places her hope in God, not in any human being.

Sarah submitted to her husband because she trusted God. Her inner spirit was (literally) "undisturbed." She gave up her desire to control, and lost her fear because she knew the Lord was looking out for her. Read 1 Peter 3:1-5.

- How is a quiet, undisturbed spirit demonstrated?

- Is that a quality of your life? Is it a worthy goal for all of us to seek?

- The woman in Proverbs 31:25 trusted deeply in God and put her hope in Him. What was her attitude toward the future?

D. Ultimately our submission is to God.

A friend of mine tells of how she learned that submission to authority is ultimately submission to God. She had gone to Salzburg, Austria, as a summer missionary. It turned out that her missionary activity was cleaning the "loos" in a three-story chalet that served as a summer camp for 40 children. When she wasn't cleaning toilets, she was peeling potatoes and slaving in a hot kitchen. What kept her motivated was the thought that with each swipe of the toilet brush, or each peel of the potato, she was serving God. There will be some situations like this in your marriage where submission is not easy. But if you have a strong, healthy motive for submitting (obedience to Christ), you can learn to humbly serve and do your best.

Our culture tells women to be aggressive, to tear down their husbands, and to make any decision they like, regardless of who it affects (just watch any sitcom on TV for proof). Satan would love for Christian women to act this way, too, because it would give him easy access to our marriages.

• How does imitating the culture make us vulnerable to Satan?

Some Practical Suggestions from Older Women
Pray for your husband. One husband gets nervous the minute he hears that his wife has "given up" on their disagreement and is praying. When you enlist God's help in any situation, you are leaving it in the right Person's hands. Watch out! God may change you instead of your husband.
Speak grace words, not death words. Be careful with your criticism, sarcasm, and hurtful words. It is better to leave things unsaid if you can't say it nicely. Praise him for the good decisions he makes. Bear in mind, he is ultimately accountable to God for his choices, as are we for our submission. Ask God to reveal to him areas of his life that need to be more Christlike. *Let no unwholesome word proceed from your mouth, but only such a word as is good for edification according to the need of the moment, so that it will give grace to those who hear. (Ephesians 4:29)* Kind words are characteristic of a wise woman. Jesus spoke graciously (Luke 4:22)—we should, too.
Focus on God's love and sovereignty, not on your troubles. Think *big* picture. Back up a few steps and look at the system God put in place. Marriage roles are His design. It's not all about you, regardless of what the world is saying. Genesis 3:16 reads, "To the woman He said, 'I will greatly multiply your pain in childbirth, in pain you will bring forth children; yet your desire will be for your husband, and he will rule over you.'" This means that women often try to usurp the leadership of the family. When we insist on our way and refuse to do it God's way, our rebellion and pride are showing. We are quenching the Spirit's leading.
Trust God – He will meet your needs. Your heavenly Father knows what you need (Matthew 6:32), and you are precious to Him (Isaiah 43:4). He describes His care for us in that your name is engraved in His palm (Isaiah 49:16). Christ modeled this by turning His situation over to His Father (Luke 23:43). Jesus entrusted Himself to the Father.

Summary

Submission means we don't demand our own way. We refuse to be self-centered. This is no easy task. In fact, humans have been rebelling against authority since the days of Eden. Like Charles Spurgeon said, "It takes more grace than tongue can tell to play the second fiddle well." Yet God asks wives to glorify Him by loving and respecting their husbands. It brings glory to Him. Even Jesus submitted to authority, and He asks us to follow His humble, selfless example. Can we do anything less?

Prayer

Heavenly Father, give us grace to submit well. Thank You for not treating us as our sins deserve. Keep us from the sin of complaining about our husbands. May we never become bitter or begrudging. Show us how to be satisfied with You and content with the leader you have placed over us. Remind us how to turn each situation over to You. Thank You for meeting all of our needs. Give us a quiet and peaceful heart which is precious in Your sight. Amen.

Notes

[1] Eugenia Price, *God Speaks to Women Today* (Grand Rapids, MI: Zondervan Publishing House, 1964), pp. 19-20.

[2] Gien Karssen, *Her Name is Woman* (Colorado Springs, CO: NavPress, 1975), pp. 31-32.

[3] Cynthia Heald, *Loving Your Husband* (Colorado Springs, CO: NavPress, 1989), p. 69.

[4] Elisabeth Elliot, *Let Me Be a Woman* (Wheaton, IL: Tyndale House Publishers, 1976), pp. 144, 153.

[5] Charles R. Swindoll, *Strike the Original Match* (Grand Rapids, MI: Zondervan Publishing House, 1993), p. 49.

[6] Timothy Keller, *The Meaning of Marriage* (New York, NY: Dutton, 2011), p. 178.

[7] John Piper and Wayne Grudem, *Recovering Biblical Manhood and Womanhood* (Wheaton, IL: Crossway Books, 2006), p. 35.

WOMANOFGRACE

Be hospitable, serving one another as good stewards of the grace of God.

Christ Calls Us to Hospitality

Do not neglect to show hospitality to strangers, for by this some have entertained angels without knowing it. (Hebrews 13:2)

Practicing grace by providing spiritual and physical refreshment to those whom God brings into our lives, generously sharing our heart, food, and home.

Introduction

Definition of hospitality: *The reception and entertainment of guests or strangers with liberality and kindness.*

This lesson is the culmination of our study of the Titus 2 woman. You have been confronted with various character traits that wives should be putting into practice. We've also discussed a woman's responsibility to love her husband and children and to make her home a place of refuge and comfort for her family. In this section, we learn about using our homes as instruments of hospitality. In the Greek language, *hospitality* means "a love for strangers." We find examples of hospitality throughout the Bible, especially in the New Testament. In the early church, hospitality was a distinctive mark of the Christian community. Believers ate together, they met for worship and fellowship, and they shared their material possessions with each other. The home was a natural base for spreading the gospel message, and hospitality provided necessary help to traveling evangelists and church teachers. Hospitality played a key role in the early expansion of Christianity.

> *Beloved, you are acting faithfully in whatever you accomplish for the brethren, and especially when they are strangers; and they have testified to your love before the church. You will do well to send them on their way in a manner worthy of God. For they went out for the sake of the Name, accepting nothing from the Gentiles. Therefore we ought to support such men, so that we may be fellow workers with the truth. (3 John 5-8)*

When Jesus sent His disciples into Jewish villages to preach the gospel, He told them not to take any supplies—no food, no luggage, no money, not even a change of clothes. He said to them, "Wherever you enter a house, stay there until you leave town," (Mark 6:8-10). They were to depend entirely on the hospitality of those who welcomed them.

- How do these verses enlarge your understanding of why hospitality was so important to early Christianity?

Biblical Foundation

> *Be hospitable to one another without complaint. As each one has received a special gift, employ it in serving one another as good stewards of the manifold grace of God. (1 Peter 4:9-10)*

- What do you think it means to practice hospitality without grumbling or complaining?

- Why do we grumble and complain about hospitality?

Some people seem to have an innate ability to practice hospitality easily, for others it is a struggle. While hospitality may be difficult, it *is* a command.

- Realizing this, what is one area of hospitality in which you would like to grow?

Do not forget to entertain strangers, for by so doing some people have entertained angels without knowing it. (Hebrews 13:2 NIV)

Read Genesis 18:1-15.

- What preparations did Abraham and Sarah make for their unexpected guests?

- How were these preparations difficult?

- How were they costly?

- One of their guests was very special. Who was He?

Lot entertained two angels (Genesis 19), Gideon prepared a feast when the angel of the LORD visited him (Judges 6), and Samson's parents encountered the angel of the LORD (Judges 13).

We most likely will never have the opportunity to entertain angels or welcome the Lord Jesus Christ to our home. But Jesus, when speaking of the future judgment, spoke these words in Matthew 25:35-40:

"For I was hungry, and you gave Me something to eat; I was thirsty, and you gave Me something to drink; I was a stranger, and you invited Me in…Then the righteous will answer Him, 'Lord, when did we see You hungry, and feed You, or thirsty, and give You something to drink? And when did we see You a stranger, and invite You in?"…The King will answer and say to them, 'Truly I say to you, to the extent that you did it to one of these brothers of Mine, even the least of them, you did it to Me."

- To whom, then, should we show hospitality?

If anyone has material possessions and sees his brother in need but has no pity on him, how can the love of God be in him? Dear children, let us not love with words or tongue but with actions and in truth. (1 John 3:17-18 NIV)

- How may we discern if we truly have the love of God living in our hearts?

- In this case, do "actions truly speak louder than words" to the world around us?

- In thinking about hospitality, to whom do our homes and possessions ultimately belong?

Betty Huizenga says:

Sometimes we can be enslaved by our homes and possessions. We become too concerned with the impressions our homes will make on others. Or we worry too much that things might get broken if we, or our children, entertain. We forget that the most important thing is to use our homes and possessions for their intended purpose, which is to share the love of Christ with others. But when we become aware that everything belongs to God, we can entertain with attitudes of thankfulness and joy! It is very freeing![1]

- What do the following verses have in common?

  I am not saying this because I am in need, for I have learned to be content whatever the circumstances. (Philippians 4:11 NIV)

  Keep your lives free from the love of money and be content with what you have, because God has said, "Never will I leave you; never will I forsake you." (Hebrews 13:5 NIV)

- Are you satisfied with what God has provided you? Why or why not?

- What does this have to do with hospitality?

The New Testament gives these qualifications for its church leaders:

An overseer, then, must be above reproach, the husband of one wife, temperate, prudent, respectable, hospitable... (1 Timothy 3:2)

Rather he must be hospitable, one who loves what is good.... (Titus 1:8 NIV)

- What is required of men who desire spiritual leadership in the church?

- How may a spiritual leader influence his family to pursue hospitality?

- How would it enhance his ministry to the congregation?

- If God would call your husband to spiritual leadership in the future, would he be qualified in this area?

- Even if your husband is not called to ministry, how does hospitality apply to him?

In her book, *Open Heart, Open Home*, Karen Mains states: "For some, like myself, hospitality is as natural as breathing. For others, the practice must be acquired. For all, the gift must be nurtured. [...] Essential to hospitality is the open heart which results in an open house." Hospitality to her is a way of life, it is her passion. The premise of her book is that "...if Christians would open their homes and practice hospitality as defined in Scripture, we could significantly alter the fabric of society. We could play a major role in its spiritual, moral and emotional redemption. For the Christian, hospitality is not an option."[2]

I firmly believe that opening your heart to those around you who need a touch of love is the first step in beginning a ministry of hospitality.

- What is your biggest fear about having guests in your home?

- How might you remedy that fear?

We need to realize that what the world calls *entertaining* is vastly different from biblical hospitality. What our society pictures is a beautiful house and table, gourmet food and drink, the perfect hostess and conversation, expensive furnishings, etc. The following chart contrasts that view with Christ-honoring hospitality. We should keep in mind the differences as we continue our discussion.

Entertaining	Hospitality
• Focuses on things • Expects payment or payback • Is modeled in *Better Homes & Gardens* • Is a matter of pride (being the perfect hostess or having the perfect meal) • Shows off what you have	• Focuses on people • Wants no payment (reward is in Heaven) • Is modeled in Scripture • Is a matter of grace (freely giving for the benefit of others) • Shares what you have

In his book *The Hospitality Commands*, Alexander Strauch states:

> *Hospitality demands old-fashioned hard work. It may be costly and is often inconvenient. It is time consuming. It places a strain on the family. Sometimes guests abuse their Christian brothers' and sisters' hospitality. And during times of persecution, hospitality can even be dangerous. Hospitality, therefore, is a concrete, down-to-earth test of our fervent love for God and His people. Love can be an abstract, indistinct idea; hospitality is specific and tangible. We seldom complain about loving others too much, but we do complain about the inconveniences of hospitality. Hospitality is love in action. Hospitality is the flesh and muscle on the bones of love. Through caring acts of hospitality, the reality of our love is tested.*[3]

- Have you ever been in a situation where it was both inconvenient and difficult to be hospitable? What did you do?

- Were there any lasting blessings from your obedience to the command?

Helpful Hints for Hospitality

1. When you are just beginning to have people in your home, start small with just dessert or snacks the first time. Later, try a simple meal with a few guests. Next, prepare a simple meal for more guests or a party. For a larger group, ask others to contribute to the meal (e.g. salad or dessert). Kids can be wonderful guests.

2. Keep ingredients in the pantry, refrigerator, or freezer for an emergency meal such as a casserole, salad, bread, and simple dessert.

3. Choose a menu where you can prepare some items ahead of time, so that everything doesn't have to be done at the last minute.

4. Think ahead. Plan your menu (being sure to ask if there are food allergies or intolerances). Shop for the groceries you will need. Prepare items in advance (desserts, salads, breads, etc.). Do last minute touch-up cleaning and remove clutter. Set the table. Get out serving dishes and serving utensils. Begin cooking food. Tidy up the kitchen and sink. Greet your guests. Enjoy!

5. Coordinating with your family, plan dates that would be available for you to entertain friends, family, and other guests. When you don't plan ahead, your good intentions usually slip through the cracks and don't get done. "If you fail to plan, you are planning to fail," said Benjamin Franklin.

6. Think about people you would like to invite to your home—visitors to church, singles, military members, church speakers, missionaries, widows, neighbors, co-workers—whomever the Lord lays on your heart. Make a plan to include them on your guest list.

7. Begin collecting recipes that your family likes, that are easy to prepare, and that you feel comfortable cooking. Practice new recipes *before* you serve them to company.

8. Think of ways to be prepared for occasional overnight guests.

9. Think about how hospitality can also include taking a meal to someone in need or taking cookies to a new neighbor.

Despite the difficulties, the extra time and work, and the inconveniences that come with hospitality, there are blessings to be reaped, some with eternal consequences. Here are just a few benefits:

1. Your children will see giving and sacrifice firsthand. It will cause them to learn to think of others who are needy, lonely, without friends and family, or in a difficult time of life.

2. People can be counseled, hurts can be healed, friendships can be started, hope can be given, prayers can be offered, and the love of Christ can be demonstrated.

3. Children can be exposed to missionaries and other church speakers in an informal setting where they can learn about different cultures and the work of Christ in the world.

4. The body of Christ is blessed when Christians learn to love and care for one another.

5. Marriages can be saved through counseling and examples of Christian husbands and wives living out their God-given roles.

6. Lives and careers can be changed, souls can be saved, life-long sins can be confessed and forsaken, eternal destinies can be altered.

7. There can be as many blessings to the one who practices hospitality as there are to those who receive it. Obedience to Christ's commands brings eternal rewards.

Summary

In closing, remember that hospitality is God's plan for His people in this world. Begin at whatever stage you are in life. Do it however you can, on your own budget, with your own limitations, in whatever venue you choose. Make a plan that suits you and your family. Blessings will flow to you, to the body of Christ, and to the world. Jesus will be glorified.

Prayer

Lord, give us a vision of how we can open our hearts and homes to those around us that need a special touch of Your love and care. May we be willing to use the resources that You have given us to further Your kingdom and bring You glory. Amen.

Notes

1 Betty Huizenga, *Apples of Gold* (Colorado Springs, CO: Cook Communications, 2000), p. 98.

2 Karen Burton Mains, *Open Heart, Open Home* (Elgin, IL: David C. Cook Publishing, 1976), pp. 19, 21-22.

3 Alexander Strauch, *Hospitality Commands* (Colorado Springs, CO: Lewis and Roth Publishers, 1993), p. 38.

Recipes

BREAD

Basic Scones

2 cups flour
6 tablespoons butter
1 tablespoon baking powder
1/2 cup buttermilk

2 tablespoons sugar
1/2 teaspoon salt
Lightly beaten egg

Mix dry ingredients. Cut in 6 tablespoons butter until mixture resembles coarse cornmeal. Make a well in the center and pour in buttermilk. If you don't have buttermilk, use regular milk. Mix until dough clings together and is a bit sticky—do not over-mix. Turn out dough onto a floured surface and shape into a 6- to 8-inch round about 1 1/2-inch thick. Quickly cut into pie wedges or use a large round biscuit cutter to cut circles. The secret of tender scones is a minimum of handling. Place on ungreased cookie sheet, being sure the sides of scones don't touch each other. Brush with egg for a shiny, beautiful brown scone. Bake at 425° for 19 to 20 minutes, or until light brown.

Cottage Cheese Rolls

1 1/2 cup cottage cheese
1/2 teaspoon baking soda
1/2 cup water
2 cups whole wheat flour
1/4 cup brown sugar
1 tablespoon or 1 package active dry yeast

1 1/2 teaspoon salt
2 eggs (heated in glass dish set in bowl of hot water)
2 tablespoons butter
1 1/2 cup bread flour

Heat the cottage cheese, water, sugar, salt, and butter on med-high heat on stovetop, stirring often. When very warm, pour into mixing bowl. Add one cup of the whole wheat flour and the baking soda, and gently stir this into the liquid. Allow the baking soda to fizz a few minutes.

Meanwhile, break the eggs into a small glass dish. Pierce the yolks and set the dish into a bowl of hot water.

To the mixing bowl now add the second cup of whole wheat and the yeast. With dough hook, beat on low for about 3 minutes. Add the warmed eggs and beat another minute or so. Gradually add the bread flour with mixer on low setting. Continue kneading with machine or by hand as you work in the flour and the dough remains soft but not sticky. Cover bowl and set on rack on top of pot with hot water or on a heating tray on low setting. Let rise one hour. Form into 16 large rolls or 24 small rolls. Place on greased pans using solid shortening or Bakers Joy. Let rise in oven on lowest setting for 10 minutes. Turn off heat for the rest of 30 minute rise.

Remove pans from oven and preheat to 350°. Bake one pan of rolls at a time for 20 to 25 minutes. Cool the rolls on racks. For optimum freshness, freeze the rolls and heat on defrost setting in microwave.

Easy Twistie Rolls

1 package Pillsbury biscuits (10 biscuits)
4 tablespoons melted butter or margarine (1/2 stick)
Sesame seeds

Twist each biscuit into a knot (looks like a pretzel). Lay biscuits on a cookie sheet, a few inches apart. Spoon melted butter over the top of each biscuit. Then sprinkle sesame seeds onto each biscuit. Bake biscuits in preheated 400° oven for about 15 minutes or until lightly browned. Let cool for a few minutes before putting them in basket or serving bowl (this lets the butter soak in a little more). You may double or triple this recipe easily—30 will fit on a large baking sheet.

Italian Bread Bowls

2 1/2 cups warm water
2 (1/4 ounce) envelopes active dry yeast
2 teaspoons salt
2 tablespoons vegetable oil

7 cups all-purpose flour
1 tablespoon cornmeal
1 tablespoon water

Stir together 2 1/2 cups water and yeast. Let stand 5 minutes. Stir in salt and oil. Add flour gradually, beating until soft dough forms.

Turn dough out onto a floured surface; knead 4-6 minutes. Place in a lightly greased bowl, turning to grease top. Cover and let rise 35 minutes or until doubled.

Punch dough down and divide into 8 equal portions. Shape each portion into a 4-inch round loaf. Place loaves on lightly greased baking sheets sprinkled with corn meal. Cover and let rise 35 minutes until doubled in bulk.

Stir together egg white and 1 tablespoon water. Brush over loaves.

Bake at 400° for 15 minutes. Brush with remaining egg mixture and bake 10-15 minutes more or until golden brown. Cool on wire racks. Makes 8 bowls. Cut a 1/2-inch slice from top of each loaf; scoop out centers leaving 3/4-inch thick shells. Fill bread bowls with soup.

Freezes well up to one month.

Egg Bread

Ingredients	Small	Medium	Large
Water	1/4 cup	1/4 cup	1/4 cup
Milk	1/4 cup	1/4 cup	1/4 cup
Eggs (room temp)	1	2	3
Butter (room temp)	1 tablespoon + 1 teaspoon	2 tablespoons	2 tablespoons + 2 teaspoons
Salt	1 1/2 teaspoons	2 teaspoons	2 1/2 teaspoons
Sugar	1 tablespoon + 1 teaspoon	2 tablespoons	2 tablespoons + 2 teaspoons
Bread flour	2 1/4 cups	3 cups	4 cups
Active Dry Yeast	1 1/2 teaspoons	2 1/4 teaspoons	1 tablespoon

Bread Machine Method: Have liquid ingredients at 80° F and all others at room temperature. Place ingredients in pan in the order specified in your owner's manual. Select basic cycle and medium/normal crust. Do not use the delay timer.

Mixer Method: Using ingredient amounts listed for medium loaf, combine yeast, 1 cup flour, and other dry ingredients. Combine water and milk; heat to 120° to 130° F.

Handheld Mixer Method: Combine dry mixture, liquid ingredients, and butter in mixing bowl on low speed. Beat 2 to 3 minutes on medium speed. Add eggs; beat 1 minute. By hand, stir in enough remaining flour to make a firm dough. Knead on floured surface 5 to 7 minutes or until smooth and elastic. Use additional flour if necessary.

Stand Mixer Method: Combine dry mixture, liquid ingredients, and butter in mixing bowl with paddle or beaters for 4 minutes on medium speed. Add eggs; beat 1 minute. Gradually add remaining flour and knead with dough hook(s) 5 to 7 minutes until smooth and elastic.

Food Processor Method: Put dry mixture in processing bowl with steel blade. While motor is running, add eggs, butter, and liquid ingredients. Process until mixed. Continue processing, adding remaining flour until dough forms a ball.

Rising, Shaping, and Baking: Place dough in lightly oiled bowl and turn to grease top. Cover; let rise until dough tests ripe. Turn dough onto lightly floured surface; punch down to remove air bubbles. Roll or pat into a 14x7 rectangle. Starting with shorter side, roll up tightly, pressing dough into roll. Pinch edges and ends to seal. Place in greased 9x5 loaf pan. Cover; let rise until indentation remains after touching. Brush loaf with slightly beaten egg mixed with 1 tablespoon water. Sprinkle with sesame or poppy seeds. Bake in preheated 375° oven 30-40 minutes. Remove from pan; cool. Makes 1 loaf.

Coconut Banana Raisin Muffins

1 2/3 cups flour
1/4 cup sugar
2 teaspoon baking powder
1/2 teaspoon salt
1/2 cup plus 2 tablespoons sliced almonds
1 1/3 cups coconut
1/2 cup raisins

2 small bananas, chopped (1 1/2 cups)
1 egg
1/2 cup milk
1/4 cup and 2 teaspoons brown sugar
5 tablespoons margarine, melted
1/4 teaspoon cinnamon

Mix flour, sugar, baking powder, and salt. Stir in 1/2 cup almonds, 1 cup coconut, and raisins. Mix in bananas. Beat egg, milk, 1/4 cup brown sugar, and 3 tablespoons margarine. Add to flour mixture. Mix until moistened. Put mixture into 12 greased muffin pans. Mix remaining coconut, 2 tablespoons almonds, 2 tablespoons margarine, 2 teaspoons brown sugar, and cinnamon. Sprinkle evenly over the muffins. Bake at 375° for 25 minutes or until done. If muffins brown too quickly, cover with foil. Makes 1 dozen muffins.

BREAKFAST/BRUNCH

Baked Scrambled Eggs

12 eggs
2/3 cup milk
1/2 teaspoon salt (or to taste)
1/8 teaspoon pepper

1/4 pound shredded cheddar cheese
1/2 pound sausage, browned

Mix first 4 ingredients well. Stir in cheese and sausage. Pour into greased 9x13 pan. Bake for 30 minutes at 350° or until knife inserted in center comes out clean. Optional: Serve salsa on side.

Breakfast Before

8 slices white bread (crusts removed)
1 pound sausage
1 cup cheddar cheese
6 eggs

2 cups milk
1 teaspoon salt
1/2 cup melted butter

Cube bread and place in bottom of 9x13 buttered pan. Brown and drain sausage; layer over bread. Layer cheese on top. Beat eggs, milk, and salt. Pour over all. Drizzle butter over all. Cover and refrigerate overnight. Bake at 350° for 45-60 minutes. Serve hot.

Blueberry Stuffed French Toast

12 slices bread in 1 inch cubes
8 ounces cream cheese in 1 inch cubes
1 cup blueberries

12 eggs
2 cups milk
1/3 cup orange juice

Put half bread cubes in 9x13 pan. Scatter cream cheese over bread, then blueberries. Add rest of bread. Whisk egg, milk, juice together and pour over bread. Chill overnight. Bake at 350°, 30 minutes covered and 30 minutes uncovered until puffed up and golden. Serve with syrup.

Cream Cheese, Celery, and Walnut Sandwiches

1/4 pound cream cheese, room temperature
1/4 celery heart, very finely chopped
1/4 cup diced walnuts

White or whole-wheat bread
Parsley sprigs (for garnish)

In a small bowl, beat cream cheese until smooth. Mix in celery and walnuts. Make sandwiches with cheese mixture. Trim off crusts of bread and cut sandwiches into rectangles or triangles. Garnish plate with sprigs of parsley.

Cucumber Sandwiches

Peel cucumbers and slice very thin. Sprinkle slices with salt and drain on paper towels. Spread white bread with unsalted butter and a thin layer of cream cheese and layer cucumbers no more than 1/4-inch high. Cut into desired shapes.

German Pancakes (Crepes)

1 3/4 cup milk
1 1/2 cup flour

3 large eggs
1/4 teaspoon salt

Put all ingredients together in blender and mix well. Stop to scrape sides at least once. Heat griddle on medium to medium high heat or electric skillet to 375°. **Should brown in 1 1/2**

minutes first side and about 1 minute second side. Serve with fresh, sugared fruit or cooked fruit, or spread with butter and sprinkle with sugar and roll up and cut in half. A favorite with my husband and kids.

Impossible Pie (A simple egg dish)

1 1/2 cups milk
3 eggs
1/2 to 1 teaspoon quiche spice (sage, oregano)
1 cup grated cheese

7 tablespoons flour
Ham, sausage, cooked spinach, cooked broccoli, or other ingredients that you like
Salt and pepper to taste

Blend milk, eggs, spices, and flour in blender. Mix in cheese and other optional ingredients. Pour into greased 9-inch pie pan. Bake at 350° for about 1 hour until set and cooked in the center.

Moist Cinnamon Apple Coffee Cake

2 cups sugar
1/2 cup oil
2 eggs
2 teaspoons cinnamon
1/4 teaspoon salt

1 teaspoon baking soda
3 cups flour
3 cups diced apples (I like Granny Smith apples for tartness)
1 cup chopped nuts (optional)

Combine sugar and oil; blend well in mixer. Add eggs and blend. Sift together cinnamon, salt, baking soda, and flour. Add gradually to sugar and oil mixture. Mix with spoon, **not mixer**. Dough will start to get stiff, so finish mixing with hands. Add nuts and apples; mix with wooden spoon. Spoon into 9x13 pan; bake at 350° for 1 hour. Cool and sprinkle top with sugar. Serve with whipped topping.

Nutty French Toast

12 slices French Bread
8 eggs
2 cups milk
2 teaspoons vanilla
1/2 teaspoon ground cinnamon

3/4 cup butter
1 1/2 cup brown sugar
3-4 tablespoons dark corn syrup
1 cup chopped walnuts

Place bread in a greased 13x9x2 baking dish. In a large bowl beat eggs, milk, vanilla, and cinnamon. Pour over bread. Cover and refrigerate overnight. Remove from refrigerator 30 minutes before baking. Meanwhile, cream butter in mixing bowl. Brown sugar and syrup until smooth. Spread over bread. Sprinkle with nuts. Bake uncovered at 350° for 1 hour or until golden brown. Yield 6-8 servings.

Potluck Eggs Benedict

1 pound fresh asparagus, trimmed
3/4 cup butter or margarine
3/4 cup all-purpose flour
4 cups milk
1 can (14-1/2 ounces) chicken broth

1 pound cubed fully cooked ham
1 cup (4 ounces) shredded cheddar cheese
8 hard-cooked eggs, quartered
1/8 teaspoon cayenne pepper
10 to 12 biscuits, warmed

Cut asparagus into 1/2-inch pieces, using only tender parts of spears. Cook in a small amount of boiling water until tender, about 5 minutes; drain. Set aside to cool. Melt butter in a saucepan; stir in flour until smooth. Add milk and broth; bring to boil. Cook and stir for 2 minutes. Add ham and cheese; stir until the cheese melts. Add eggs, salt, cayenne, and asparagus; heat through. Serve over biscuits. Yields 10-12 servings.

DESSERT

Chocolate Velvet Cheesecake

CHOCOLATE CRUMB CRUST

1-2 tablespoons unsalted butter at room temperature
1 package (8 1/2 ounces) chocolate wafer cookies finely ground
Pinch of salt and cinnamon
1/3 cup unsalted butter, melted and cooled to room temperature

Coat bottom and sides of 9-inch springform pan evenly with unmelted butter. Mix cookie crumbs, salt, and cinnamon in medium bowl. Drizzle melted butter over crumb mixture. Stir and toss mixture vigorously with fork until slightly darkened and uniform. Press crumb mixture evenly on the sides and bottom of the springform pan. Refrigerate for 30 minutes.

CHEESECAKE

12 ounces semisweet chocolate broken into small pieces
2 tablespoons unsalted butter
1 1/2 pounds cream cheese, room temperature
1 1/2 cups whipping cream
1 teaspoon vanilla
1 cup granulated sugar
3 large eggs at room temperature, slightly beaten
2 tablespoons unsweetened cocoa powder

Fresh strawberries if desired
Powdered sugar

- Place oven rack in center. Preheat oven to 350°.
- Combine chocolate and butter in top of double boiler. Place over hot, but not simmering water. Cook over low heat until chocolate is completely melted. (I use the microwave to melt the chocolate.) Stir chocolate mixture until smooth. Reserve at room temperature uncovered.
- Cut cream cheese into 1-inch cubes. Place in large mixing bowl. Beat at medium speed, scraping down sides of bowl as needed until completely smooth. Gradually beat in chocolate mixture until uniformly colored. Continue beating while gradually adding cream and vanilla. Beat until blended.
- Continue beating cheese mixture at medium speed while very slowly adding granulated sugar, beat until sugar is absorbed. Add eggs about 1/4 cup at a time, beating well and scraping down sides. Pour cocoa powder over batter, beat at low speed until cocoa is thoroughly incorporated.
- Pour batter into cold unbaked chocolate crumb crust. Spread top smooth. Gently rotate pan several quarter turns to settle batter. Bake 30 minutes. Reduce oven temperature to 325°. Continue baking 30 minutes longer. Turn oven off. Let cake stand in oven with door ajar for 30 minutes.
- Transfer pan to wire rack away from drafts. Let cool undisturbed until sides and bottom of pan are completely cooled to room temperature. Remove sides of pan. Refrigerate cake uncovered overnight or at least 8 hours. Cover cake loosely with plastic wrap. Refrigerate until serving time. Just before serving, sprinkle powered sugar lightly over cake. Serve with strawberries if desired. Serves 8-12.

Cheesecake

GRAHAM CRACKER CRUST
18 graham crackers finely crushed
1/2 cup melted butter
3 tablespoons sugar

Mix together and press into a 9-inch pie pan.

TOPPING
1 cup sour cream
3 1/2 tablespoons sugar
1 teaspoon vanilla

Mix together and spoon onto cake.

CHEESECAKE
12 ounces cream cheese
2 teaspoons vanilla
2 eggs beaten
2 teaspoons lemon juice
3/4 cup sugar

Whip cream cheese and combine beaten eggs, sugar, vanilla, and lemon juice. Beat until light and frothy. Pour into graham cracker crust and bake in 350° oven for 15-20 minutes. Cool for 5 minutes, then spoon topping onto cake, beginning from outer edge. Bake 10 minutes longer. Cool, then refrigerate at least 5 hours before serving.

Cherry Blueberry Delight

CRUST
2 cups flour
1/2 cup dark brown sugar
1 cup margarine
1 cup chopped nuts

FILLING
1 (8 ounce) package cream cheese
1 teaspoon vanilla
1 cup margarine
1 cup chopped nuts
1 cup powdered sugar
8 ounces Cool Whip

TOPPING
2 cans pie filling (cherry and/or blueberry)

Mix crust like pie dough, cutting margarine into flour and brown sugar. Add chopped nuts and press into 9x13 pan. Bake 15 minutes at 400°. Use fork to crumble baked crust into pieces and leave in pan. Mix cream cheese, powdered sugar, and vanilla. Cream well. Fold into Cool Whip. Spread over cooled crust. Pour two cans pie filling over top. (May use all one type, or make 1/2 cherry and 1/2 blueberry dividing down the center with foil.) Chill at least 12 hours. Keeps for several days.

Coconut Lemon Meltaways

Dry Ingredients
1 1/2 cups almond flour
1 1/2 cups dried shredded unsweetened coconut
1/3 cup coconut flour
2 big pinches of salt

Wet Ingredients
6 tablespoons Agave or Grade B maple syrup or raw organic honey
4 tablespoons lemon juice
2 teaspoons vanilla
1 tablespoon lemon zest

Thickener
1/4 cup and 1 tablespoon melted coconut oil

Mix dry ingredients and set aside. Stir the wet ingredients together. Pour dry ingredients into electric mixer. With the mixer on, slowly stream the wet ingredients.

Thickener - While mixer is on, stream in the melted coconut oil. Batter will thicken fairly quickly as it mixes with the oil and the oil cools down. Form cookies into 1-inch balls and place on a pan.

Option 1 - Warm under a dehydrator or oven (set it at its lowest heat, leaving the door cracked open). Warm the cookies for 1 hour, maybe a bit longer. Finished cookie will be dry on the outside and melt-in-your-mouth moist on the inside. Place cookies in the fridge after they have cooled down, letting them chill and set before eating.

Option 2 - Place cookies to set/chill in the fridge for about an hour. If you opt not to heat/dry cookies, the texture will be soft and moist.

Chocolate Tunnel Cake

Deep chocolate cake mix
Hershey's chocolate syrup

8 ounces Cool Whip
Chocolate sprinkles

Follow high altitude directions for a deep chocolate cake mix using a Bundt pan. When cool, slice the top off, being careful to keep it unbroken. Scoop out a small tunnel in the remaining cake. (Keep the broken pieces to mix with Cool Whip as a separate dessert.) Mix Hershey's chocolate syrup with Cool Whip to make a light chocolate flavor. Spoon mixture into tunnel, replace top of cake and frost with the remaining Cool Whip. Sprinkle chocolate sprinkles on top.

Fortune Cookies

3 egg whites
3/4 cup sugar
1/2 cup butter, melted and cooled
1/4 teaspoon vanilla

1/4 teaspoon almond
1 cup flour
2 tablespoons water

Melt butter and set aside to cool. Prepare fortunes to be placed inside cookies. Preheat oven to 375°. Grease cookie sheet or line with parchment paper. In a glass or metal bowl, whip egg whites and sugar on high until frothy (approx. 2 minutes). Reduce speed to low. Stir in butter, vanilla, almond, water, and flour one at a time, mixing well after each addition. Consistency should resemble pancake batter. Spoon into 3-inch circles, 4 at a time, being careful not to let the batter get too thick. Leave room for spreading. Bake 5-7 minutes or until edges begin to brown slightly. Quickly remove one at a time, place message in the center. Fold in half. Fold ends of half together to a horseshoe shape. Place cookies in a muffin tin to cool until set.

Mock Devonshire Cream

1/2 cup heavy cream or 8 ounces softened cream cheese
2 tablespoons confectioner's sugar
1/2 cup sour cream

In a chilled bowl, beat cream until medium-stiff peaks form, adding sugar during the last few minutes of beating. (If you are using cream cheese, just stir together with sugar.) Fold in sour cream and blend. Makes 1 1/2 cups.

Triple Chocolate Fudge Cake

1 small package chocolate pudding mix (not instant)
1 box chocolate cake mix (dry mix)

1/2 cup semisweet chocolate pieces
1/2 cup chopped nuts
Whipped cream

Cook pudding as directed on package and blend dry cake mix into hot pudding. Mixture will be thick. Pour into prepared 13x9 pan and sprinkle with chocolate pieces and nuts. Bake 30 to 35 minutes at 350°. Cool 5 minutes; cut into 2-inch squares and arrange on cake plate or a tray covered with doilies. Serve plain or topped with a dollop of whipped cream.

Gluten-Free Dessert: Berries and Vanilla Cream

Assortment of fresh berries (blueberries, strawberries, blackberries, raspberries) or other fruit (peaches)
2 large eggs
1/4 cup sugar
2 tablespoons plus 1/2 teaspoon cornstarch
Pinch of salt
1 cup whole milk (or fat free half and half) plus extra
1/2 teaspoon pure vanilla extract

1. Whisk yolks until smooth. Mix sugar, cornstarch, and salt in a medium saucepan over medium heat. Add milk in a slow, steady stream. Cook, stirring until mixture begins to bubble and thicken.
2. Pour 1/3 of milk mixture into yolks, whisking constantly. Return mixture to saucepan, and cook over medium heat, stirring often. As it thickens, pour in enough milk so that it remains soupy rather than thick like a pudding. Stir in vanilla.
3. Refrigerate until cold.
4. Mix berries or other fresh fruit in a bowl. Pour vanilla cream over fruit.
5. For a non-gluten free alternative, make pancakes filled with fruit and use as a substitute for syrup. Fresh pineapple and toasted coconut pairs with this well.

Cranberry Bliss Bars (Starbucks copycat)

Bars	Frosting	Topping
1 cup butter (2 sticks), very soft	3 ounces cream cheese, softened	1/3 cup Craisins, chopped
1 cup brown sugar	2 tablespoons butter, softened	1-2 tablespoons grated orange rind
1/3 cup granulated sugar	3 cups confectioner's sugar	1/3 cup white chocolate chips
3 large eggs	2 teaspoons orange extract (or vanilla)	1/2 teaspoon canola oil
2 teaspoons orange extract (or vanilla)		
2 cups flour		
1 1/2 teaspoons baking powder		
1 teaspoon ground ginger		
3/4 cup Craisins (dried cranberries)		
3/4 cup white chocolate chips		

[Lighter Version: Omit half the butter (1/2 cup). Omit 1/2 cup brown sugar. Add 1/2 cup applesauce and 1/2 cup brown sugar Splenda mix.]

1. Preheat oven to 350° (325° for a glass or dark pan). Prepare a 9x13 pan (or 10x15 pan) by lining it with parchment paper or use a nonstick spray.
2. Bars: With an electric mixer, beat together butter and sugars until fluffy; add eggs and orange extract and beat until combined.
3. Add the flour, baking powder, and ginger and beat briefly. Add cranberries and chips, stirring just to blend and being careful not to over-mix.
4. Spread thick batter in prepared pan and bake at 350° (23-24 minutes for 10x15, 27 minutes for 9x13), until the edges are light brown and a skewer inserted into the center comes out mostly clean. Let it cool completely.
5. Frosting: Blend cream cheese and butter until fluffy. Add orange extract and confectioner's sugar and beat until frosting is fluffy and spreadable (adding 1 teaspoon milk if needed). Spread evenly over cooled bars.
6. Garnish: Use a zester to remove rind from an orange. Chop 1/3 cup Craisins coarsely. Sprinkle this garnish or orange zest and Craisins over frosted bars.

7. For the final topping, mix white chocolate and oil in a glass measuring cup. Microwave 60% power for 1 minute; stir. Repeat 1 more minute at 60% power; stir. Use a fork to drizzle the white chocolate in thin diagonal strips across bars.
8. Allow one hour for the white chocolate to set before cutting. (To make signature Starbucks triangles, cut jelly roll pan into 20 large squares. Then cut each square in half diagonally.)

PIES

Pie Crust

1 1/2 cups flour
1 teaspoon salt
1/2 cup shortening
4-6 tablespoons water

Blend flour and salt. Cut in shortening. Add water gradually until dough holds together without crumbling, yet not too moist. Place on floured surface and roll to desired size. This is a single piecrust. For pies requiring a top crust, you will need to double this recipe using a flour to shortening ratio of 3-to-1.

Apple Pie

3-5 cups sliced apples
3/4 cup sugar
2 tablespoons flour
1 teaspoon cinnamon

1 tablespoon lemon juice (optional)
1 tablespoon butter (optional)

Mix sugar, flour, cinnamon, and lemon juice. Mix in apples. Place in pie shell. Dot with butter. Make lattice crust and flute the edges. Bake at 425° for 10 minutes, then at 375° for 30 minutes.

Cherry Pie

1 cup sugar
2 tablespoons flour
1 tablespoon butter

3 cups pitted cherries
1/2 cup cherry juice
1 tablespoon lemon juice

Mix together sugar and flour. Put 1/3 of the mixture in pan containing piecrust. Add cherries and juice. Add remaining sugar mixture and cover with lemon juice and butter. Make a top lattice crust and flute the edges. Bake at 425° for 10 minutes, then at 375° for 30-50 minutes (done when juice bubbles are thick).

Blackberry Pie

2 pints blackberries
1 cup sugar
1/4 cup flour
1/4 teaspoon cinnamon

1/8 teaspoon nutmeg
2 tablespoons butter
1 tablespoon milk
1 tablespoon lemon juice (optional)

Mix sugar, flour, cinnamon, and nutmeg. Mix with blackberries. Spread in piecrust. Dot with butter. Put on top crust (lattice or solid with hole cut in top). Brush with milk and sprinkle with sugar. Bake at 400° for 40-45 minutes or until juice bubbles through steam vent and crust is golden brown.

Peach Pie

3 packages frozen peaches
1/4 cup flour
1 teaspoon lemon juice

1/4 teaspoon cinnamon
1/2 cup sugar
2 tablespoons butter

Mix peaches and lemon juice. Mix sugar, flour, and cinnamon; stir into peaches. Put in 9-inch pastry-lined pie pan. Dot with butter. Cover with top crust and flute the edges. Cover edge with 2-3-inch slip of aluminum foil to prevent excessive browning. Remove foil during last 15 minutes of baking. Bake at 425° for 30-45 minutes or until crust is brown and juice begins to bubble through slits in crust.

Jo's Easy Berry Pie

Makes 2 pies. Gather about 8 cups of frozen berries (or add some fresh). Add 1 cup water; simmer on stovetop on low/med heat until melted and easy to stir. Increase heat to med/high and stir in 1 cup sugar. Bring to a bubbling boil. Mix together 1/4 cup cornstarch and 1/2 cup water, stir into boiling mixture, continue to stir another minute or two until thickened. Pour into two baked and cooled pie crusts. Chill at least 3 hours. Serve with whipped cream or vanilla ice cream. (Can also be made with Splenda for a low-cal dessert.)

Lemon Meringue Pie

Use 9-inch baked shell
1 1/2 cups sugar
1/3 cup plus 1 tablespoon cornstarch
1 1/2 cups water

3 egg yolks, slightly beaten
3 tablespoons butter or margarine
2 teaspoons grated lemon peel
1/2 cup lemon juice

Bake pie shell. Heat oven to 400°.

Mix sugar and cornstarch in medium saucepan. Gradually stir in water. Cook over medium heat, stirring constantly, until mixture thickens and boils. Boil and stir 1 minute. Gradually stir half of mixture into beaten egg yolks. Blend into hot mixture in pan. Boil and stir 1 more minute. Remove from heat. Stir in butter, lemon peel, and lemon juice. Pour into baked pie shell. Heap with meringue, carefully spreading to edge of crust to prevent shrinking or weeping. Bake about 10 minutes until delicate brown. Cool away from draft.

Meringue

3 egg whites

1/4 teaspoon cream of tartar

6 tablespoons sugar

1/2 teaspoon vanilla

Beat egg whites and cream of tartar until foamy. Beat in sugar, 1 tablespoon at a time. Continue beating until stiff and glossy. Do not under-beat. Beat in vanilla.

Classic Pie Pastry

2 cups all-purpose flour

3/4 teaspoon salt

2/3 cup shortening

6-7 tablespoons cold water

In a small bowl, combine the flour and salt; cut in the shortening until mixture is crumbly. Gradually add water, tossing with a fork until a ball forms. Cover and refrigerate for 30 minutes or until easy to handle.

Cut dough in half so that one ball is slightly larger than the other. Roll out larger ball on a lightly floured surface to fit a 9- or 10-inch pie plate. Transfer pastry to pie plate. Trim pastry even with edge of plate. Add filling. Roll out remaining pastry to fit top of pie; place over filling. Trim, seal and flute edges. Cut slits in top. Bake according to the pie recipe directions.

Never-Fail Pie Crust

2 cups all-purpose flour

1/2 teaspoon salt

2/3 cup shortening

1 tablespoon white vinegar

5-6 tablespoons milk

In a small bowl, combine the flour and salt; cut in shortening until mixture is crumbly. Sprinkle with vinegar. Gradually add the milk, tossing with a fork until a ball is formed. Cover and refrigerate for 30 minutes or until easy to handle.

Divide pastry in half so that one ball is slightly larger than the other. Roll out large ball on a lightly floured surface to fit a 9- or 10-inch pie plate. Transfer pastry to pie plate. Trim pastry even with edge of plate. Add filling. Roll out remaining pastry to fit top of pie; place over filling. Trim, seal and flute edges. Cut slits in top. Bake according to whatever pie recipe directions you are using.

Oil Pastry

2 cups all-purpose flour

1 1/2 teaspoons salt

1/2 cup salad oil

4-5 tablespoons cold water or milk

In a small bowl, combine the flour and salt. Pour salad oil and cold water or milk into measuring cup (but do not stir). Add all at once to the flour mixture. Stir lightly with fork. Form into ball; flatten slightly.

Divide in half. Roll first half between two 12-inch squares of waxed paper. First dampen table or counter slightly so paper won't slip. Roll to fit 9- or 10-inch pie plate. Peel off top sheet of paper and fit dough, paper side up, into pie plate. Trim pastry even with edge of plate. Add filling. Roll out remaining pastry to fit top of pie; place over filling. Trim, seal and flute edges. Cut slits in top. Bake according to recipe directions.

MAIN DISHES

Baked Potato Soup

2 large potatoes	3 cups milk
1/4 teaspoon salt	1/3 cup flour
3 tablespoons sliced green onion	1/4 cup shredded cheese
1/4 teaspoon pepper	1/4 teaspoon dill weed
1/3 cup butter	Bacon crumbled

Bake potatoes and scoop out pulp. Cook 3 tablespoons onion in butter until tender. Stir in flour, dill weed, salt, and pepper. Add milk all at once. Cook and stir until bubbly and thickened. Cook 2 minutes more. Add potato pulp and 1/4 cup cheese and stir until cheese melts. Garnish with cheese, green onions, and bacon. Only makes about 3 big bowls; may need to double recipe.

Chicken Corn Potato Chowder

About 6 cups water	5-6 potatoes, peeled and diced
2 cans corn with juice	Salt, pepper, and celery to taste
4 split chicken breasts	1 onion diced
2 cups milk	1 tablespoon parsley

Cook chicken in water until chicken is completely cooked. Remove chicken and strain the broth. Return broth to pan with cut up potatoes. Cook potatoes and onions in the broth while peeling chicken off the bone. Take a potato masher and partially mash the potatoes in the broth before adding remaining ingredients. Then add chicken, corn, milk, and seasonings. Do not boil soup, but simmer for 30 minutes. If soup needs thickening, mix water and flour together and add to soup. Makes a big pot. Optional: Add Mrs. Dash, pepper, and crumbled bacon on top.

Quick White Chili

Sauté: 1 teaspoon minced garlic, 1 cup onion (chopped), and 1 teaspoon olive oil for 5 minutes.

Add: 1 cup cooked chicken (cut up), 2 cups chicken broth, 2-15 ounce cans Northern beans, 1 can diced green chiles (4 ounces or 7 ounces), 2 tablespoons fresh cilantro (or 1 teaspoon dry), 1 teaspoon oregano, 1/2-1 teaspoon cumin, 1/4 teaspoon cayenne pepper.

Heat 15 minutes, until bubbly. Serve in bowls garnished with grated cheese, sour cream, salsa, and/or broken tortilla chips. (For chicken broth, I boil the chicken, save the water I used, and add 1-2 bouillon cubes.)

Clam Chowder

1 cup water	1/2 to 1 tablespoon dried minced onion
8 ounce can minced clams (reserve juice)	2 cups cubed potatoes
1 chicken bouillon cube or granulated powder	2-3 medium carrots diced

Put the water, reserved juice from clams, bouillon, potatoes, carrots and the minced onions together into 3 quart pot. Start on medium high until boiling and then on low for 20 to 30 minutes.

1 10-ounce can cream of celery soup
1 1/4 to 1 1/2 cups milk
8 ounces coarsely grated Monterey jack cheese
1/2 tablespoon dry parsley flakes or 2 tablespoons fresh, diced

Turn heat to medium and add the celery soup, milk, grated cheese, parsley, and the reserved clams. Stir and heat till the cheese is melted. Serves 4 to 5 people.

Mum's Special Chicken Soup

1 broiler-fryer chicken (3-1/2 to 4 pounds)	1 garlic clove
3 quarts water	2 1/2 teaspoons salt, optional
1 medium onion, quartered	1/2 cup thinly sliced carrots
4 celery ribs	1/2 cup chopped fresh parsley
2 chicken bouillon cubes	cups cooked rice
2 parsley sprigs	

Place chicken and water in a large kettle or Dutch oven; bring to a boil. Reduce heat; add onion, celery, bouillon, parsley sprigs, garlic, and salt, if desired. Cover and simmer until the chicken is tender, about 1 hour. Remove chicken; allow to cool. Strain and reserve broth; discard vegetables. Add carrots to broth and simmer until tender, about 15 minutes. Debone chicken;

cut into cubes. Add chicken and chopped parsley to broth; heat through. Ladle into bowls; add rice to each bowl. (I usually put the rice into the soup instead of into each bowl.)

Basic Crepe

1 3/4 cups milk	1/4 teaspoon salt
1 1/2 cups flour	3 tablespoons butter, melted
3 large eggs	

Combine flour and salt, add remaining ingredients and blend well with a blender or hand mixer. Cover batter and chill for 30 minutes. Heat a small nonstick pan. Add butter to coat. Pour about 1/4 cup batter into the center of the pan and swirl to spread evenly. Cook for 30 seconds and flip, cook approximately 30 seconds more or until both sides are light brown. Lay flat to cool. (Crepes can be made ahead of time. After cooling, stack crepes, separating each with wax paper. Place in a Ziploc bag. Crepes can stay in the refrigerator for two days or up to two months in the freezer.)

Chicken Broccoli Crepes

1-10 ounce package frozen cut broccoli	2 tablespoons flour
1/4 teaspoon ground nutmeg	3/4 cup shredded Swiss cheese
2 tablespoons butter	1/4 teaspoon salt
1 1/2 cups milk	2 cups finely chopped cooked chicken

Cook broccoli according to package, drain, and set aside. For sauce, melt butter in medium saucepan. Blend in flour, salt, and nutmeg. Add milk all at once. Cook and stir until thickened and bubbly. Cook, stirring constantly for 2 minutes more. Add Swiss cheese, stir until melted, set aside.

For filling, combine chicken, broccoli, and 1 cup of the cheese sauce. Spoon about 1/2 cup filling along center of unbrowned side of each crepe. Place crepe on plate. Top with a little cheese sauce. Sprinkle with paprika or sliced almonds if desired.

If you want the crepes to be ready all at once in a casserole style: Roll up the crepes, place seam side up in baking dish. Pour remaining cheese sauce over crepes. Sprinkle with paprika if desired. Cover and bake in 375° oven for 18-20 minutes. Serve with sliced almonds if desired.

Southwest Chicken Crepes

2-3 chicken breasts, cut up	3 tablespoons butter
1/2 onion, diced	4 tablespoons flour
1 clove garlic, diced	1 3/4 cups milk

1/4 teaspoon each salt, pepper and cayenne pepper

1/2 cup shredded cheddar cheese

1/2 cup salsa

Black beans (canned)

Sauté chicken breasts, garlic, and onions in olive oil over medium heat until chicken is cooked through. In saucepan over medium heat, melt butter. Add flour and whisk. Whisk in milk and seasonings. Simmer over low heat for about 5 minutes until thickened. Stir in cheese and salsa and heat sauce for about 5 minutes on low heat. Place crepes on a work surface. Spoon chicken and beans onto crepe. Add sauce and additional grated cheese if desired. Roll crepe. Serve with black beans. Top with cheese and salsa as you like.

Chicken Salad (Perfect to Serve a Friend for Lunch)

1 1/2 cups cooked Uncle Ben's Long Grain and Wild Rice

1 large apple diced (use green apple, if possible, for color)

2 cups cooked chicken cut into bite size chunks (4 boneless chicken breasts raw)

1 cup mayonnaise

1 cup cut up grapes (use red grapes, if possible, for color)

1 tablespoon lemon juice

1 cup celery diced (optional)

Boil chicken for about 30 minutes on stove. (You may cook it ahead and freeze the chicken.) Let cool and put in the refrigerator. Chicken is much easier to cup up into pieces when it is cold. Cook the long grain rice and let it cool, then place it into the refrigerator. I usually do these two steps the night before I am going to serve the chicken salad. The morning that you are going to serve the salad, cut up your chicken and dump it into a bowl. Dump all other ingredients into the bowl and stir together. Place the salad into your serving bowl. Sprinkle the top of the salad with Season-All Salt for an elegant presentation. You may line club crackers around the outside of the serving bowl and add a sprig of parsley in the center. Lay leaves of lettuce on your plate and top with the salad. Serve with either hot rolls or crackers.

Deep Dish Pizza

1 box Pillsbury Hot Roll Mix (plus 2 tablespoons flour)

1 tablespoon vegetable oil

1 1/4 cups warm water

1 pound mozzarella cheese, grated

1 jar (14 ounces) Ragu pizza sauce

Pepperoni, sausage, toppings

1. Generously grease large pizza pan (or cake pans). Preheat oven to 425°.
2. Make dough, using Hot Roll Mix, yeast packet, flour, warm water and oil. Mix in mixer for 5 minutes (or knead by hand for at least 5 minutes).

3. Pat dough into pizza pan. Generously prick dough with fork. Cover with towel. Let rise about 30 minutes.
4. Uncover dough. Spread half of cheese on top of dough, then the pizza sauce. Top with other half of cheese.
5. Add meat and/or toppings.
6. Bake at lowest oven rack position for about 20 minutes or until cheese is melted.

Easy Enchiladas

15-16 flour tortillas
1 1/2 pounds hamburger, browned
1 large chopped onion
1-4.5 ounce can green chilies
1 large can refried beans

1-14.5 ounce diced tomatoes, drained
1 cup grated cheddar cheese
2-10 ounce cans enchilada sauce
2/3 cup grated cheddar cheese

Spread tortillas on the counter. Brown hamburger; add onions and cook until clear. Add and heat green chilies, tomatoes, refried beans, and 2/3 cup cheese. Put approximately 1/2 cup mixture on each tortilla. Roll and place in greased pans: one 9x13 and one 7x10. Pour enchilada sauce over tortillas. Sprinkle cheese over top. Cover with foil. Bake at 350° for 45 minutes. Serve over shredded lettuce with sour cream and salsa. Freezes well. For more guests, serve with salad and Spanish rice.

Grilled Chicken Salad

Yields six servings as main course
6 chicken breast halves, skinned and boned
9 cups mixed salad greens
6 cups assorted fresh fruit
1 1/4 cups honey lime dressing (see below)
1 1/4 cups roasted pecan pieces (bake 10-15 minutes at 350° on cookie sheet)

Grill chicken breasts over an outdoor grill until thoroughly cooked; set aside to cool. (I cooked boneless breasts in the oven for 40 minutes at 400°.) Divide salad greens evenly among 6 plates. Cut cooled chicken into slices and arrange over greens. Top each salad with 1 cup fruit (blueberries, strawberries, cantaloupe, honeydew melon, pineapple, kiwi, red grapes, or apples...no watermelon) and 1/4 cup honey lime dressing. Garnish with pecan pieces.

Honey Lime Dressing

1/4 cup sugar
1/4 cup honey

1 tablespoon dry mustard
1 1/2 teaspoons ground ginger

3 1/2 tablespoons fresh lime juice

3 1/2 tablespoons water

3/4 cup olive or vegetable oil

Combine sugar, honey, mustard, ginger, lime juice, and water in a blender. Blend for 30 seconds. Slowly add oil in steady stream. Continue to blend until well combined.

Hot Chicken Salad

2 cups cooked chicken, diced

1 cup mayonnaise

2 cups chopped celery

2 tablespoons lemon juice

1/2 teaspoon salt (or less)

1 tablespoon grated onion

1/8 teaspoon pepper

1/2 cup chopped almonds

1/2 cup grated cheddar cheese

Combine above ingredients. Add 1/2 cup grated cheddar cheese on top. (As an option, add 1 cup crushed potato chips as well.) Bake 10 to 15 minutes at 450°.

Loin of Pork

3 to 4 pound loin pork roast

1 teaspoon oil

2 teaspoons dry leaf marjoram

14 ounces peach halves (reserve 1/2 cup juice)

1/4 cup sugar and dash of salt

1/2 teaspoon dry mustard

1 teaspoon paprika

2 teaspoons cornstarch

2 tablespoons vinegar

Rub oil on the roast using pastry brush and rub with marjoram. Roast 1 1/2 hours and then remove from oven to score fat on the roast. Roast another 1 to 1 1/2 hours till meat thermometer is 170°. Roast at 325°.

GLAZE: Combine sugar, mustard, paprika, cornstarch, and salt. Mix these together in a skillet. Add vinegar and 1/2 cup peach juice. Cook on medium high, stirring constantly until sauce becomes clear and thick. Spoon onto roast, which has been drained. Next arrange paper towel dried peaches around the roast and fill each cavity with chili-sauce. Bake another 15 minutes. Remove roast from oven and wait 10 minutes until carving.

Spinach Strawberry Salad

9 cups baby spinach

1 pint fresh strawberries, halved

1/2 cup slivered almonds, toasted

Dressing:

1/4 cup vegetable oil

2 tablespoons sugar

1 tablespoon chopped onion

1 teaspoon poppy seeds

1 teaspoon sesame seeds

1/4 teaspoon paprika

1/8 teaspoon Worcestershire sauce

In a large bowl, combine the spinach, strawberries, and almonds. Place dressing ingredients in a blender; cover and process until combined. Pour over salad and toss to coat. Serve immediately. Yield: 6-8 servings.

Taco Salad

1 can tomato soup

1 can kidney beans

1 can ranch style beans

1 pound ground beef (90% lean)

1 package taco seasoning

1 cup water

Brown the beef in hot skillet. Drain both cans of beans and add to beef along with the tomato soup, taco seasoning, and the water. Bring to boil on medium high heat stirring constantly. Simmer for 30 minutes, stirring occasionally. Serve over corn chips. Delicious piled on with steamed rice, chopped tomatoes and lettuce, taco sauce, sour cream, shredded cheese, etc.

Peasant Pot

8 medium zucchini, cut lengthwise and cubed

6 large, very ripe tomatoes; peeled (or use 2 cans Italian plum tomatoes, 28 ounce size)

2/3 box D'Italian (Ronzoni) pasta (or other small pasta) cooked a little less than directed

2 or 3 large onions sliced thinly

1 large clove garlic, diced

2-3 tablespoons oil

1 large bay leaf

2 teaspoons each, basil and oregano

2 teaspoons salt

2 cups beef stock (may use bouillon)

2 cans dark kidney beans

Sauté onions and garlic until soft. Add mashed tomatoes and steam until juicy. Add spices. Add soup stock. Add liquid from kidney bean cans. Add sliced zucchini and simmer until lightly turning color, then lower heat. Add kidney beans and pasta just before serving. Heat through. More water may be added to make it thinner as desired. Adjust seasonings to your taste.

Stir Fry

5-6 chicken breasts (debone and slice into small bite-size pieces)
1 large onion, cut up
4-5 ribs celery
4-5 carrots

Mushrooms
Small package frozen peas (thawed)
Pea pods or other fresh vegetables (zucchini, water chestnuts, red pepper, etc.); sliced
Cooked rice

Chop all ingredients. Make sure that you chop chicken on a different chopping surface than the vegetables. You may use a wok or an electric fry pan. Stir fry your chicken bits in about 1 tablespoon peanut oil that has been heated. Remove chicken from heat. Throw in all your vegetables except the mushrooms and peas. If the vegetables begin to stick, add a small amount of water. Toss the vegetables until about half done. Add the mushrooms and the thawed peas. When the vegetables are still crispy, add the chicken back into the pan. When done, place lid on pan while you serve the rice. Add the vegetables on the rice. Do *not* continue to cook the vegetables and chicken mix. The veggies are supposed to be crispy. You may add soy sauce if you like. Choose vegetables for your stir fry that your family will eat.

You can buy or make sauces that will make the vegetable/chicken mix taste sweet, tangy, etc. By making it this way, you will taste the vegetables, and it is very nutritious.

SIDE DISHES

Pressure Cooker Brown Rice

(Makes 3 1/2 cups)
1 tablespoon olive oil
1/2 cups short or long-grain brown rice

2 1/2 cups boiling water
3 3/4 teaspoon salt

In pressure cooker, heat the oil over medium-high heat. Add the rice and cook, stirring frequently, for 2 minutes or until lightly browned. Turn off the heat and stir in the boiling water and salt (watch out for sputtering oil). Cover, lock the lid in place, and turn the burner to high. Bring the pot to high pressure. Adjust the heat to maintain high pressure and cook for 15 minutes. Turn off the heat and let the pressure drop on its own while the rice steams for another 5 to 10 minutes. Reduce any remaining pressure with a quick release method under a cold tap. Remove the lid, tilting it away from you to allow any excess steam to escape. If the rice is not sufficiently cooked, stir in a few tablespoons of boiling water. Replace the lid without locking it. Simmer over very low heat for another 1 to 2 minutes or until done. Fluff the rice with a fork before serving.

Twice Baked Potato

12 huge baking potatoes
2 cups shredded cheddar cheese
2-3 sticks butter (not margarine)
Milk

24 ounces light sour cream
Salt and pepper
1 pound bacon

Wash baking potatoes and bake until not quite done (fork pushes in, but not easily). Potatoes will continue to cook when removed from oven. Let cool, then slice in half lengthwise. Carefully scoop out potato, being careful not to go too close to skin or puncture skin. Mash potatoes with a hand masher first to mash up large chunks. Add butter and sour cream and use mixer to blend completely. Add salt, pepper, and milk to mixture until mixture can be scooped back into shells but is not runny. Top with cheddar cheese. Cook bacon until *crispy* and drain completely. Crumble and add to top of potatoes. Heat at 350° until cheese just barely begins to melt and potatoes are warmed thoroughly. It took me about 1/2 hour with all 24 huge halves heating in oven. Serve hot.

Evaluations

Mentor

NAME: _____

1. What did you enjoy the most about the program?

2. What did you enjoy the least about the program?

3. How would you say the ladies responded to the mentors? To the program?

4. Which lesson(s) did you teach?

5. Which foods did you cook at your house?

6. Would you like to be involved again in this program? If so, when? What is your best time of year?

7. How did you feel about your financial contribution to the program — providing the food you prepared and the food for the banquet? Was this a financial burden for you?

8. How did you like the banquet? Any suggestions to make it better?

Participant

NAME: _____

1. What did you enjoy most about this program?

2. What did you enjoy least?

3. Do you think this is a worthwhile program? Why?

4. How did you personally respond to the mentors?

5. Which lesson did you enjoy the most? From which lesson did you learn the most? Which lesson was the hardest for you? Why?

6. How did you like the banquet? Did you like having the husbands there?

7. How did you like the menus and recipes that were demonstrated? Which was your favorite?

8. If an opportunity came for another program to be offered, could you volunteer to help in any way? Babysitting? Clean-up? Serving for the banquet?

9. Any additional comments:

Sources & Recommended Reading

Ardizzone, Carol. *Motherhood, The Proverbs 31 Ministry.* 1-877-P31-HOME.

Barnes, Marilyn Gwaltney. *Love (and Baby Powder) Covers All: A Daily Survival & Devotional Guide for Mothers of Young Children.* Joy Publishing, 1992.

Bourke, Dale Hanson. *Everyday Miracles, Holy Moments in a Mother's Day.* Word Publishing, 1989.

Briscoe, Stuart and Jill. *The Family Book of Christian Values.* Colorado Springs, CO: Alive Communications, Inc., 1995.

Briscoe, Jill and Judy Golz. *Space to Breathe, Room to Grow.* Wheaton, IL: Victor Books, 1985.

Brown, Anne. *Principles For Parents: A Bible Study.* Junction City, KS, 1978.

Bruner, Kurt and Otis J. Ledbetter. *The Heritage.* Chicago, IL: Moody Press,1996.

Campbell, Ross. *How to Really Love Your Child.* Colorado Springs, CO: Chariot Victor Publishing, 1980.

Chapman, Gary & Ross Campbell, M.D. *The Five Love Languages of Children.* Northfield Publishing, 1997.

Chapman, Gary. *Love as a Way of Life.* New York, NY: Doubleday, 2008.

Christenson, Evelyn. *What Happens When We Pray for our Families.* Colorado Springs, CO: Chariot Victor Publishing, 1992.

Coble, Betty J. *Woman - Aware and Choosing.* Nashville, TN: Broadman Press, 1975.

Coloroso, Barbara. *Kids Are Worth It! Giving Your Child the Gift of Inner Discipline.* New York, NY: William Morrow, 1994.

Daigle, Kay. "God's Design for Building Your Marriage: Submission," www.bible.org.

Decker, Barbara. *Proverbs for Parenting.* Lynn's Bookshelf, 1973.

Dillow, Linda. *Calm My Anxious Heart: A Woman's Guide to Finding Contentment.* Colorado Springs, CO: NavPress, 2007.

Dillow, Linda and Lorraine Pintus. *Intimate Issues.* Colorado Springs, CO: WaterBrook Press, 1999.

Dillow, Linda. *Satisfy My Thirsty Soul.* Colorado Springs, CO: NavPress, 2007.

Dobson, Dr. James. *Bringing Up Girls.* Carol Stream, IL: Tyndale House, 2010.

Dobson, Dr. James. *Dr. Dobson Answers Your Questions about Raising Children.* Carol Stream, IL: Tyndale House, 1986.

Dobson, James. *Parenting Isn't for Cowards.* Waco, TX: Word Books, 1987.

Dobson, Dr. James. *The New Dare to Discipline.* Carol Stream, IL: Tyndale House, 1992.

Dobson, James. *The Strong-Willed Child*. Carol Stream, IL: Tyndale House, 1992.

Eggerichs, Emerson. *Love & Respect*. Nashville, TN: Thomas Nelson, 2004.

Elliot, Elisabeth. *Let Me Be a Woman*. Wheaton, IL: Tyndale House Publishers, 1976.

Ethridge, Shannon. *Every Woman's Battle*. Colorado Springs, CO: Waterbrook Press, 2003.

Ethridge, Shannon and Stephen Arterburn. *Every Young Woman's Battle*. Colorado Springs, CO: WaterBrook Press, 2004.

Faber, Adele and Elaine Mazlish. *How to Talk So Kids Will Listen & Listen So Kids Will Talk*. New York, NY: Avon, 1982.

Feldhahn, Shaunti. *For Women Only*. Sisters, OR: Multnomah Publishers, 2004.

Fleming, Jean. *A Mother's Heart*. Colorado Springs, CO: Nav Press, 1982.

George, Elizabeth. *A Woman's High Calling*. Eugene, OR: Harvest House Publishers, 2001.

Goodin, Rev. Douglas. notes from a marriage seminar at Front Range Alliance Church.

Harris, Gregg & Joshua. *Uncommon Courtesy for Kids*. Noble Publishing Associates, 1990.

Hartley, Hermine. *The Family Book of Good Manners*. Bristol Park Books, 1994.

Heald, Cynthia. *Loving Your Husband*. Colorado Springs, CO: NavPress, 1989.

Huizenga, Betty. *Apples of Gold*. Colorado Springs, CO: Cook Communications, 2000.

Hunt, Susan. *Spiritual Mothering*. Wheaton, IL: Crossway Books, 1992.

Johnson, Spencer, M.D. *The One Minute Mother*. New York, NY: William Morrow, 1995.

Karssen, Gien. *Her Name is Woman*. Colorado Springs, CO: NavPress, 1975.

Kopp, David & Heather. *Praying the Bible for Your Children*. Colorado Springs, CO: WaterBrook Press, 1971.

Ledbetter, J. Otis and Gail. *Heritage Builders: Family Fragrance*. Colorado Springs,CO: Chariot Victor Publishing, 1998.

MacArthur, John. *The Family*. Chicago, IL: Moody Press, 1982.

Mahaney, Carolyn. *Feminine Appeal*. Wheaton, IL: Crossway Books, 2004.

Mains, Karen Burton. *Open Heart, Open Home*. Elgin, IL: David C. Cook Publishing, 1976.

Mattson, Ralph, and Thom Black. *Discovering Your Child's Design*. Elgin, IL: David C. Cook Publishing, 1989.

Moore, June Hines. *You Can Raise a Well-Mannered Child*. Broadman & Holman Publishers, 1996.

Morley, Patrick. *What Husbands Wish their Wives Knew about Men*. Grand Rapids, MI: Zondervan Publishing Co, 1998.

Mouser, Barbara. *Five Aspects of Woman*. Waxahachie, TX: International Council for Gender Studies, 1998.

Ortlund, Anne. *Children are Wet Cement*. Fleming H. Revell Co., 1981.

Piper, John. *Desiring God*. Colorado Springs, CO: Multnomah Books, 1986.

Piper, John, and Wayne Grudem. *Recovering Biblical Manhood and Womanhood*. Wheaton, IL: Crossway Books, 2006.

Price, Eugenia. *God Speaks to Women Today*. Grand Rapids, MI: Zondervan Publishing House, 1964.

Ross, Autumn Ellis. "A Life Worthy of the Calling." Wheaton College Alumni Magazine, Fall 2007.

Schaeffer, Edith. *What is a Family?* Old Tappan, NJ: Fleming H. Revell Company, 1975.

Smalley, Gary and Greg Smalley. *Bound By Honor*. Colorado Springs, CO: Focus on the Family, 2002.

Strauch, Alexander. *Hospitality Commands*. Colorado Springs, CO: Lewis and Roth Publishers, 1993.

Swindoll, Charles. *Growing Strong in the Seasons of Life*. Grand Rapids, MI: Zondervan Publishing House, 1983.

Thomas, Gary. *Sacred Influence*. Grand Rapids, MI: Zondervan Publishing House, 2004.

Trent, Dr. John. *My Mother's Hands, Celebrating Her Special Touch*. Colorado Springs, CO: WaterBrook Press, 2000.

Trent, John & Cindy, and Gary & Norma Smalley. *The Treasure Tree: Helping Kids Understand Their Personality*. Nashville, TN: Thomas Nelson, 1998.

Trent, John. *The Two Trails: Helping Kids Get Along and Enjoy Each Other*. Nashville, TN: Thomas Nelson, 1997.

Tripp, Tedd. *Shepherding a Child's Heart*. Shepherd Press, 1984.

Way, Tim. *Above All Else: Directions for Life - Women*. Grand Rapids, MI: Family Christian Press, 2006.

WOMANOFGRACE

Called to Mentor

Foreword

Anne Brown

We older women have an important role to play in the lives of younger women. No one can take our place!

I have been involved in several mentoring programs over the last 15-20 years. When my husband and I ministered together in our first church, I began teaching and training the young women there. I was only thirty years old at the time, but I was considerably older than many of the newly married military wives in the congregation. I taught several Bible studies that included principles of Christian womanhood and the training of children.

I did not feel qualified, but I had such a burden for the young women in our church that I decided to do it, trusting God to empower me in my ignorance and weakness. It wasn't until much later in my life that I realized that mentoring is a command (Titus 2:3-5). I discovered that although there are many ways for women to minister, this is a Spirit-inspired expectation for the mature women of the church.

All the mentoring programs I have been involved with have had a common problem—finding qualified mentors. I would discontinue one program and begin another one, often frustrated and ready to give up the idea completely. Then the Holy Spirit would quietly remind me of the scriptural command. It would be acceptable to give up a certain program, but I must never give up mentoring. God wants the older, mature women to teach and train younger women. Ultimately, it's a question of obedience.

Woman of Grace is a program based on Titus 2:3-5 designed to train young women in Christian skills and principles. Our church has used this format and its accompanying mentor training for ten years. It has been gratifying to see the response of young women in their desire to be godly wives and mothers. For some women, *Woman of Grace* has been life-changing. I pray that God will continue to use it to transform Christian women and to glorify Jesus.

Called to Mentor – Why Should We Do It?

While ministering in Crete, Paul observed that many women whose children were grown spent their days clutching together to sip wine and gossip (as was the custom in 65 AD). Later, he wrote to Titus to instruct these older women "to be reverent in their behavior, not malicious gossips nor enslaved to much wine, teaching what is good, so that they may encourage the young women to love their husbands, to love their children, to be sensible, pure, workers at home, kind, being subject to their own husbands… so that the word of God will not be dishonored" (Titus 2:3-5). Susan Hunt observes: "It is interesting that of all the ways Paul could have told the women to combat the decadence of their culture, he told them to invest their energies in training the younger women to live Christianly in their society."[1] Mature Christians, not the voices of the world, must set the standards for our lives. We should not look to the world to teach young women how to be women.

The first and primary reason we are to mentor is that God commands it. It is His plan for educating young women in godly living. It is our divine assignment. The next reason is "so that the word of God will not be dishonored." The Greek word for dishonored is *blasphemetai*. It means "to speak of with irreverence, to revile or abuse." It is a strong word from which we derive the English word *blaspheme*. Our lives should give no occasion for God to be discredited. The world is watching and carefully observing the lives of those who claim to be Christians. Does our character reflect Christ? Does our walk match our talk? Do we live differently from the world? If not, the world will discount both our words and our profession of faith.

Another reason we mentor is that women need other women. We were made for fellowship, companionship, and friendship. There is no substitute for someone who has "been there and done that" when it comes to pregnancy, birth, potty training, and the terrible twos. Women are able to help other women because they understand their many stages of life. They are well-suited to be advisors and helpful influences.

We no longer have the strong generational ties we used to have. Our children often move away, and daughters don't live close enough for their mothers to be able to assist them in valuable life skills. We live in a mobile society where there is little support from neighbors, and friendships are difficult to maintain. Women, especially, sense that loss. In *Spiritual Mothering*, Susan Hunt shares Dr. James Dobson's explanation:

> *A century ago, women cooked together, canned together, washed at the creek together, prayed together, went through menopause together, and grew old together. And when a baby was born, aunts and grandmothers and neighbors were there to show the new mother how to diaper and feed and discipline. Great emotional support was provided in this feminine contact. A woman was never really alone.*

> *Alas, the situation is very different today. The extended family has disappeared, depriving women of that source of security and fellowship. Her mother lives in New Jersey and her sister is in Texas. Furthermore, American families move every three or four years, preventing any long-term friendships from developing among neighbors.*[2]

In former times, homemaking skills were also taught as part of a girl's formal education. Many of us took home economics classes in school. Every girl was taught basic skills in cooking, meal planning, grocery shopping, babysitting, and the use of a sewing machine. There were also 4-H Clubs, Girl Scouts, Brownies, and Camp Fire Girls programs that encouraged housekeeping and other life skills. Today, many women work outside the home. There is little time to prepare meals – dinner is take-out. Children are busy with school and activities, and mom is busy helping them. The time pressures of the job along with work at home leaves little time for teaching or learning homemaking skills.

Sherilyn Jameson describes the situation well in her poem, "Where Have All the Mentors Gone?" found in *Between Women of God* by Donna Otto:

> *Where have all the mentors gone –*
> *Those Titus 2 women of the past,*
> *Those older, God-fearing role models?*
> *Where have all the mentors gone?*
>
> *Maybe you've gone to seek fulfilling careers.*
> *Maybe you've gone to self-awareness classes.*
> *Maybe you're busy staying fit –*
> *Playing tennis or at aerobics.*
> *Or maybe you're just taking time for yourselves –*
> *Going to lunch, playing bridge, or shopping at the mall.*
>
> *Wherever you have gone, we've missed you.*
> *Our generation has indeed missed you.*
> *We need you.*
> *Maybe more than any generation of mothers.*
> *With our vague role descriptions and society's confusing messages,*
> *Oh, how we need faithful, committed mentors.*
>
> *We need you to remind us of the value of being a stay-at-home mom*
> *and a loyal, submissive wife.*
> *We need to see the art of homemaking modeled for us*
> *over and over and over again.*
> *We need to listen to the advice of an older woman*
> *now that we know what to listen for.*
> *We need to watch you respond to the joy and sorrow of life;*
> *with the divine wisdom of God's Word;*
> *we need to see how God's promises in Scripture work out in real life.*
>
> *We need your encouragement to see the eternal picture and the benefits of following God*
> *when the day is bogging us down and clouding our view.*
> *We need your tried-and-true tips on loving our husband, raising our children,*
> *keeping our home, and living for Jesus.*
> *We need to listen and learn from the wealth of experience and wisdom*
> *you've collected during your years of living.*
> *We need you cheering us on when it seems no one is noticing or appreciating our many efforts*
> *to make our houses homes, our children saints for the King, our husband our top priority,*
> *and Jesus the love of our life.*

We need to hear your many little comments that remind us
that this exhausting stage in our life is indeed a stage and it is temporary.
We need, possibly more than anything else, a mentor in our life
who will take our name before the Father daily, beseeching His throne on our behalf.

Where have all the mentors gone?
You may have gone many different places.
But we know where a few of you are – involved with Mentors for Moms.[3]

Older women today have many valuable resources and skills, yet they are not being challenged to offer them. When I talk to women about being mentors, they respond as if they have nothing to share. But they do, and our young women desperately need their encouragement in meal planning, cooking, baking, sewing, housekeeping, time management, and raising children. Most of us have managed to prepare nourishing meals for our families over the years, even if we don't love cooking. We have learned to decorate our homes, provide clothing for our family, organize a household schedule, live within a budget, and train up our children. We have become keepers of the calendar, chauffeurs *par excellence*, and effective organizers of our family's many activities. Is a woman who has managed all of this qualified to help younger women? Yes, she is!

So, why then are so many women reluctant to be mentors? Here are some of the reasons I have encountered:

1. They are uncertain about their knowledge and abilities. They think, "What do I have to offer?" Many women who have made a career of being a full-time wife and mother think they do not have any skills worth sharing with others. That is not so! They are just the ones to encourage young women in the midst of their marriages and child-rearing responsibilities.

2. They've never been encouraged to teach someone else. Mentoring is a new concept for them. They have never been mentored themselves and don't understand the benefits to be gained by their participation in this discipline.

3. They are uncertain about their spiritual qualifications. They think that one must first become perfect before she can instruct others. If that were the case, none of us would be qualified. None of us has "arrived" spiritually. But when God calls, He empowers and equips. If you pursue a mentoring ministry, He will give the wisdom you need.

4. They think they are too busy. (Don't we all?) We need to ask ourselves, "With what am I busy?" Are we spending our life investing in eternal things, or merely passing time with things "that moth and rust will corrupt"? Do you spend your time doing things that *you* want to do or things that God wants you to do? God will hold us accountable for our use of the time and talents He has given us. Many older women whose children go off to college or move out of the home take a job to occupy their time or to pay for educational expenses. That is not wrong, if they continue using their Spiritual gifts and keep their households running smoothly, but they should also consider using some of their extra time training a younger generation of wives and mothers.

5. They think they've paid their dues. They are ready to quit activities such as Sunday school, nursery, VBS, choir, and committee chairmanships. They're ready to retire. But in God's economy, there is no retirement. There may be a change in "office hours" due to health and energy limitations, but it is never acceptable to cease serving God. Your church is a part of your spiritual family. If you don't serve, the whole church suffers. Consider how the apostle Paul spent the last years of his life. He was in jail, writing letters to young pastors and churches, preparing them to continue the work that he had begun. He is a good model for us.

6. They don't want to be looked at as *older* women. With our society's emphasis on youth, it is no wonder that women struggle with this terminology. Yet, aging is changing. Older women are breaking the mold, forging new territory, and framing new images. Now, just because you are "over the hill" does not mean that you've got "one foot in the grave."

Consider this anonymous poem shared by Donna Otto:

The Grandmother's Poem

*In the dim and distant past
When life's tempo wasn't fast
Gramma used to rock and knit,
Crochet and tat, and babysit.*

*Gramma now is in the gym
Exercising to keep slim.
Now she's golfing with the bunch,
Taking clients out to lunch,*

*Going north to ski and curl,
And all her days are in a whirl.
Nothing seems to stop or block her
Now that Gramma's off her rocker.[4]*

But even if that were not true, our standard is Scripture, not culture. Biblically, being older and mature is virtuous, a virtue that brings responsibility.

7. They are afraid to venture out into new horizons. They fear new relationships, along with the risk of sharing their lives and mistakes with strangers. Even though they understand that their time will be an investment in other women's lives, they are often afraid of the commitment. They fear that they will not be accepted or welcomed by younger women as they mentor.

There are probably other reasons to add to this list, but the fact remains that we need to be messengers of God, beacons of His light, and channels of His love. We should accept the challenge of sharing our lives with others.

What Is a Mentor?

The word mentor comes from Homer's epic, *The Odyssey*. Donna Otto states: "When King Odysseus leaves to fight in the Trojan War, he charges his trusted friend Mentor with the care of his son Telemachus and the management of the home. Mentor trained Telemachus in all the ways a father would train a son, and today we use his name to refer to a trusted counselor, guide, tutor, or coach."[5]

We use the word to mean the transferring of a specific area of knowledge, usually within the business world or trade unions. It is a purposeful, intentional, and planned sharing of wisdom based on one's life experiences. I will never forget Dr. Howard Hendricks' words to the seminary wives at Dallas Seminary. He asked us, "What am I doing today that will guarantee my impact for Jesus Christ on the next generation?" That question made an indelible mark on my future life and ministry. We see many godly examples in Scripture modeling this process: Priscilla and Aquila to Apollos, Barnabas to Paul, Paul to Titus, Paul to Timothy, Elizabeth to Mary, Naomi to Ruth, and others. This is God's plan for edifying the church and passing on the Christian faith to the next generation.

Have you ever been mentored by a mature older woman? It may not have been a structured time or formal sit-down session, but rather the simple sharing of friendship, wisdom, and life lessons from one woman to another. Or perhaps it was a structured, formal session involving teaching, prayer, and sharing. Either way, think of the blessing it was to you. You can be that kind of blessing to someone else.

I had the privilege of being mentored in Dallas, Texas, by Vickie Kraft, author of *Women Mentoring Women* and *The Influential Woman*. As I sat under her teaching for four years in a classroom setting, she imparted her love for teaching children, her love for her husband and her family, and most of all, her love for God's Word. She encouraged me to make Scripture the basis of every ministry I engaged in, an example I have attempted to follow over the years.

A mentor must be available, which takes time. And she must be vulnerable, opening up about the work God is doing in her life, willingly sharing both her failures and successes in life. It is important that she also exemplifies the faithfulness of God as she walks daily with Him. The wisdom she shares must be God's.

In another setting, I became an informal mentor for a new church friend. She participated in all the Bible studies that I taught, but we also enjoyed casual time together with our families. We played tennis, prayed with needy friends, did craft projects together, hiked through swamps looking for interesting grapevines, started a food co-op, cooked together, and became great friends. Years later when I was speaking at a ladies retreat, she told me what a great mentor I had been to her. At first I was speechless because I didn't consider the time we had spent to be mentoring. The friendship that we enjoyed became mentoring as I shared my life and wisdom with her. Informal moments, given in love, can influence another woman's life as much as the formal ones.

In *The Influential Woman*, Vickie Kraft lists ten principles demonstrated by Naomi and Ruth which give us a model for the older/younger relationship:

- The older woman must be a good role model. Her life must attract the younger woman.

- The older woman must have the right motives. She should not be seeking to meet her own needs, but trying to meet the needs of the younger woman.

- The older woman must be an encourager. She should support, praise, and admonish without obligating the younger woman to herself.

- The older woman must be an advisor, not an authority. She mustn't impose her will, but should respect the right of the younger woman to make decisions and to accept responsibility for the consequences.

- The relationship should be a mutual ministry. The younger woman has much to offer the older woman and must contribute what she can to the relationship. It should not be a one-way street.

- Communication is vital. There ought to be open, honest, and mutual communication at regular intervals for the relationship to flourish.

- Both parties have responsibilities. The older is responsible to counsel, train, and protect. The younger is responsible to be teachable, to accept counsel, and to respect the wisdom of the older.

- God's Word must be our authority. The older must instruct and advise according to God's Word and should encourage the younger to claim her blessings.

- Both parties can experience blessing.

- Such relationships will be influential in the future.[6]

Susan Hunt tells us:

"When we make an investment in younger women, we will be enriched personally, the sense of community in the local church will be deepened, society will be blessed, and God's Word will be honored."[7]

Because it is God's plan, there are many benefits. You will be blessed, and you can make a difference in a younger woman's life. Some of the benefits you may see:

- Changed lives—younger women will be given a new perspective on their role in life.

- Fellowship and friendship as you spend time together.

- Blessings from your obedience to God.

- Learning new ways of doing things—the younger learn from the older, and the older learn from the younger. (It's never too late to learn new things.)

Who Can Be a Mentor? Am I Qualified?

Titus 2:3 tells us, "Older women likewise are to be reverent in their behavior, not malicious gossips nor enslaved to much wine…." The Greek word that is used for older women is *presbutidas*, meaning "an aged or elderly woman." The implication is that these older women were spiritually qualified to model, teach, and build character into the lives of the younger, less mature women in the church. An older woman's desire should always be toward growing in wisdom so that she may share it with younger women. This wisdom should be very practical, helping with everyday problems that arise in marriage and child-rearing.

Donna Otto adds: "And when pain comes to a younger woman, an older woman can be available, willing to listen, and willing to walk alongside her. She can also, when the moment is right, offer the perspective that God uses life's hard times to draw us close to Him, refine our faith, and make us more like Christ."[8]

A mentor must seek the guidance of the Holy Spirit. The Bible is full of men and women who felt inadequate to perform their God-given task. We, too, may feel inadequate to follow Christ's plan for our lives. We should, however, be willing to be used by Him, trusting Him to enable us. We can become messengers of God's love, truths, and values to the next generation through the power of the Holy Spirit. Donna Otto shares a thought from Elisabeth Elliot: If we are going to do something for God, we first need to acknowledge our weakness and our inadequacy…. If anyone thinks she's qualified and would make a great spiritual mentor, then I'd say she's not qualified!"[9]

Paul gave specific qualifications for older women. They were to be reverent in their behavior. The King James Version translated it as "behavior as becometh holiness." Matthew Henry translated it as "one whose behavior becomes a woman consecrated to God." In ancient Greek culture, the words used pictured a pagan priestess serving in the temple of her god—a full-time service of worship.

A New Testament example of this behavior is found in the gospel of Luke. Mary and Joseph brought the infant Jesus to the temple. There they met an 84-year-old prophetess named Anna. Anna had become a widow after just seven years of marriage. From that time on, she never left the temple, serving night and day with fasting and prayers. In the New Covenant, everything in a woman's life is to be sacred, "temple service," whether teaching a Sunday school class, changing diapers, or preparing meals for her family.

A further qualification for these mature women is that they are not to be "malicious gossips." A malicious gossip is one who accuses, repudiates, gives false information, or is a talebearer. Gossip is a sin. Women in particular are susceptible to this temptation. 1 Timothy 3:11 repeats this admonition, "Women must likewise be dignified, not malicious gossips, but temperate, faithful in all things." It should be noted that a spiritual woman who desires to be a mentor should be able to keep confidences so that trust can be assured in the relationship.

The last qualification given by Paul is that the older woman should "not be enslaved to much wine." Instead of overindulging in alcohol, she fills her life with love for Christ and service to Him. Paul uses a Greek word from the *doulos* family meaning "a slave." Romans 6:17-18 states: "But thanks be to God that though you were slaves of sin, you became obedient from the heart to that form of teaching to which you were committed, and having been freed from sin, you became slaves of righteousness." How incredible! We were once slaves of sin, but now as Christians we have become slaves of righteousness. In 1 Corinthians 6:12b, Paul says, "I will not be mastered by anything." There are many things today that can enslave, not just alcohol. Overindulgence in things that seem innocent may often lead to idolatry, whether it is work, TV, shopping, talking on the phone, Facebook, or a hobby. Anything can become our master if we let it.

Who then is qualified to teach and mentor younger women? Paul's standards are high. One who walks with God and spends time studying His Word and progressing in the sanctification process. As we spend time with our Lord in prayer and in His Word, we are increasingly being conformed into His image. That is our goal.

Mentors should desire to build into the lives of younger women. There needs to be a willingness to share your life experiences (good and bad) and to be genuine with those you teach and instruct. Young women often put their mentors on a pedestal, thinking they are perfect. When you share your life experiences (even the times you failed), they are encouraged that God can bring good into our lives out of the ashes of our failure. They are encouraged that as you persevered through life's problems, you continued to grow in your Christian faith. They will be encouraged, knowing that they, too, may someday serve as a mentor to others. We are preparing the future generation to lead the church in the next twenty years and carry on the Christian faith.

The ultimate purpose for our lives is to pursue living for God's glory by exalting Jesus in everything (Colossians 1:15-18). How do we do this as mature women? I believe it means completing the mentoring work He has given us, in joyful obedience to His will. When Mary was told about the privilege of bringing the promised Messiah into the world, she joyfully replied: "May it be to me as you have said." Her response showed her clarity of purpose in obedience to her Master. What has God asked you to do to serve Him here on this earth? How can you glorify God as a mentor? Are you willing to respond as Mary did?

How We Mentor

A mentor models Christ-like character, she teaches what is good, and she encourages young women in their walk with the Lord, training them to be prudent, self-controlled, and wise.

A good mentor discovers that it takes time and discernment to do it well. It also takes a tender, caring heart. She must study her apprentices well enough to discover the needs of their hearts.

She must strive to be a good listener. First she listens, and then she seeks to give helpful advice when she has something worth giving. It will be up to the younger women to decide whether or not to implement her suggestions. You cannot change anyone. Only the Word of God and the work of the Holy Spirit will bring permanent transformation. The mentor's goal is to share what she has learned on her journey. She prays, teaches, encourages, and counsels, then looks to Jesus to bring the results.

An ideal mentor feels a sense of burden to help others strive for godliness. She is trustworthy, careful not to share with others those things that have been given to her in confidence. She is available and approachable. She is vulnerable. She is committed to the program she is using and expects the same from her trainee. She abounds in praise when her younger friend grows and shows grace when progress is slow. Most importantly, she is a faithful prayer warrior who seeks her heavenly Father on behalf of her apprentice.

We can be confident that God's eternal truth will never change. It endures from generation to generation. And He may be calling you to pass it on to the next one. You, too, can invest your life in the lives of those you mentor. You don't have to be perfect, just faithful. Will you serve? Will you help equip the next generation of the Lord's servants?

Find Us Faithful

We're pilgrims on the journey
Of the narrow road
And those who've gone before us line the way
Cheering on the faithful, encouraging the weary
Their lives a stirring testament to God's sustaining grace

Surrounded by so great a cloud of witnesses
Let us run the race not only for the prize
But as those who've gone before us
Let us leave to those behind us
The heritage of faithfulness
Passed on through godly lives

Oh may all who come behind us find us faithful
May the fire of our devotion light their way
May the footprints that we leave
Lead them to believe
And the lives we live inspire them to obey
Oh may all who come behind us find us faithful

After all our hopes and dreams have come and gone
And our children sift through all we've left behind
May the clues that they discover
And the memories they uncover
Become the light that leads them
To the road we each must find

Oh may all who come behind us find us faithful
May the fire of our devotion light their way
May the footprints that we leave
Lead them to believe
And the lives we live inspire them to obey.
Oh may all who come behind us find us faithful[10]

Our Program

Woman of Grace is a mentoring program created to follow the admonition in Titus 2:3-5 regarding the duty of older women in the church:

> *"Likewise, teach the older women to be reverent in the way they live, not to be slanderers or addicted to much wine, but to teach what is good. Then they can train the younger women to love their husbands and children, to be self-controlled and pure, to be busy at home, to be kind, and to be subject to their husbands, so that no one will malign the word of God." (NIV)*

Woman of Grace might be best described as a nurturing ministry. The word nurture means "to nourish, train, or cherish." Our mentors nurture our participants through sharing their time, talents, and life lessons. Each of the younger women should feel pampered and loved. We do not announce or promote this, but we strive to make them feel it each week from the time they step through the door until they leave. To some women, this becomes the most important day of their week as they look forward to it with much anticipation and eagerness. All meetings begin with hugs at the door from their mentors. The one complaint that we always hear from participants is that the time doesn't last long enough. One young woman exclaimed that "she could do this once a week for the rest of her life." When the session ends, tears usually fall, tissues are passed, and embraces given as we say goodbye for the last time.

Woman of Grace is a cooking ministry, seeking to bring the older and younger generations together for encouragement and friendship. Younger women tend to seek out relationships with those in their own age group. Many women enter into marriage ignorant of the skills needed in keeping their home running smoothly. They haven't been taught even the basic cooking skills. Our program is not a gourmet cooking school (although you could certainly include that in your program). The greatest need for the women in our church is instruction in meal planning and preparation, focusing on some inexpensive recipes that can be used with families and guests. We have discovered that many novice cooks are hesitant to try a new recipe if it has too many new ingredients that they would have to buy. Long, complicated recipes are also rejected because they take too much time. We also strive to teach basic principles of nutrition, and we are adding some new recipes for diabetics, vegetarians, and those that need gluten-free diets.

Woman of Grace is short, lasting only eight weeks. The first seven lessons consist of three distinct elements: instructional cooking lessons, teaching from the Word of God, and fellowship around the table as they enjoy the food they have prepared. The final meeting, which includes their husbands, is a celebration banquet. Mentors, younger women, and husbands gather to enjoy a delicious meal, followed by fun, fellowship, sharing, and a time of prayer.

~ How to Begin ~

First, you need to determine whether your church or Christian community needs encouragement and training for younger women. The next step is to choose mentors by carefully observing their character and lifestyle. If you cannot find spiritually qualified older women, pray that God will send some to you, or create a training program for potential mentors. Sometimes you find women who aspire to be mentors but who lack confidence. If that is the case, you can work with them individually until they are ready to serve. Most of your potential mentors have probably never been mentored themselves, so they are reluctant to begin mentoring others. This training will also give you the opportunity to familiarize them with the program. (It is important to understand that any program can be altered to meet the needs of your congregation and your mentors. In the ten years that we have been using our present format, we have made numerous changes and improvements. Every year is a work in progress.)

Each week we meet in the home of one of the mentors. The girls love seeing the different homes of our older women. (They sometimes even ask for a tour of the home before we start our meeting.) You will need homes that are big enough to hold a group of about ten women. We usually have six younger women and four mentors in each session.

One woman commented: "I am so grateful for our mentors. These are strong godly women who live out today's 'Proverbs 31 woman.' It's good for me to see those who have walked the road longer (and are still walking)... their advice, laughter, wisdom, etc. I loved coming into a home of fun, honest, loving and godly women every week. I was refreshed and renewed every time we met."

It works well to have three separate rooms designated for your meeting. You will need a kitchen large enough for close to ten women who will be chopping, mixing, and baking together. Usually the cooking mentor for the week will do a demonstration, asking for the help of the girls in preparing the dish to be served. You will need to have a separate dining area where the food will be eaten after the lesson is taught. Before the young women arrive, the cooking mentor has already set the table (except for the beverage, butter, cream and sugar, etc.). Designate another room for the teaching time. There should be enough seating for everyone in your group. Often chairs are moved from the teaching area to the dining area in preparation for your meal together. We eat together and discuss what was taught during the Bible study time. Specific questions are helpful to begin these table conversations.

Our meetings take place seven weeks in a row. We usually meet on a weekday morning from 9:00 a.m. to noon. We have also held sessions in the evenings to accommodate women who work during the day. One year we met on Saturday mornings, every other weekend, so that family time was not always compromised. You can decide what works best for your situation.

Babysitting may be a challenge for women with small children. It does not work well to have childcare in the same home where the meeting takes place, so we arrange for childcare using young women who have already been through the program or volunteers from the church. Some groups may choose to pay for childcare, others may require each participant to make their own childcare arrangements.

All mentors take turns teaching. (We arrange the schedule so that the cooking mentor never teaches on the same day that she does the cooking demonstration.) Each lesson is carefully written to include Scripture references for the subject to be taught. The teaching mentor also adds her own life experiences—often stories of her own failures and what God taught her through them. It is a humbling experience, but it's a vital part of being real with those you serve. The young women are given hope, seeing that other godly women know the struggle but continue to strive for obedience in their lives. We have found that these stories are an especially meaningful aspect of the meetings.

One young woman commented: "I enjoyed getting to know the mentors; it was comforting, knowing they are not perfect. As they shared their mistakes and lessons learned, it was nice to know I don't have to hide my flaws."

Prayer is at the heart of our ministry because obedience only occurs when the Holy Spirit is active. We begin praying before the participants are chosen. We ask for God's help in the selection process that He would open the hearts of our young trainees. During our first session together, we pray for the needs of everyone present. Each mentor prays weekly for the girls. Every meeting day, our mentors gather for prayer before the girls arrive. At the final banquet, we pray again for each woman and her family. Prayer continues after our mentoring program is over as the Lord brings the girls to mind. Often, even after the formal program is over, a mentor will meet with a specific woman for prayer, encouragement, or counseling.

Before a new session begins, the director chooses mentors. We have found that limiting our program to six young women is the right fit for the size of our homes. We need four mentors each time so that no one is overworked. Some mentors prefer to do the cooking demonstrations, and some prefer to teach. Every mentor hosts at least one meeting in their home. After the mentors are chosen, we have a planning meeting to decide the details: the dates for the next session, where we will meet each week, who will cook each week, what recipes will be used on which date, when the lessons will be taught, and who will teach the various lessons.

After the schedule is planned, discussion takes place regarding the young women who have been considered as participants in the program. Those selected are asked to review the meeting times, checking for any conflicts in their schedules. If a woman knows that she will miss more than one session, it is recommended that she postpone her involvement for another time. Often we have a waiting list of those who want to be involved in the training. We ask the women to agree to be faithful in their attendance and to study the lessons before coming to each meeting. We understand that there are always emergencies, but commitment is a virtue worthy of a follower of Christ.

~ A Typical Meeting ~

The girls arrive to be welcomed by a designated greeter/mentor who gives them a hug and a name tag. They mingle for about ten minutes while all the women arrive, then promptly transition to the cooking demonstration. (We have learned not to wait for latecomers because it trains the women that they do not need be on time.)

The first meeting is different from all the rest of the sessions. After the women are greeted and introduced to one another, everyone sits down at the table for coffee and a light snack. It often consists of a breakfast casserole or muffins and fruit. The conversation around the table is very informal. Then the women gather in the meeting room for a time of getting to know one another. Each participant is asked to introduce herself, tell about her family, share some of her interests and hobbies, and give one or two prayer requests. The mentors then pray for each young woman and her family, being sure to pray for those specific requests that were mentioned. After the prayer time, the study materials are handed out and the schedules for the session are explained, including the date, time, and location of the banquet. Next, the first lesson (on keeping the home) is taught by the teaching mentor. Since the women have not prepared for this lesson in advance, Scriptures are read and questions are asked. If the girls are reluctant to participate, the other mentors are ready to contribute to the conversation. The first session ends when the lesson is finished. The women are reminded to do their homework before the next session.

All the rest of the meetings (lessons two through seven) will have the same schedule. The girls arrive at 9:00 a.m. and the cooking demonstration begins about 9:10 a.m. Although the length of the cooking will vary from recipe to recipe, we usually allow about an hour. (The pie-making session always takes longer because each young woman makes her own pie to take home to her family. We adjust the timing for all of the rest of the activities accordingly.) After the cooking time, we move to the teaching session which also lasts about one hour. If the cooking time runs longer, the teaching time may also run later than usual. Generally, the conversation and eating time will take less than an hour. We end the session promptly at noon. (It is important to finish on time because the babysitters have been with the children for 3½ hours already.) Before the mentors leave, they help with cleanup, clearing the table, loading the dishwasher, putting chairs away, etc.

We sometimes alter the schedule. For example, if we prepare a dish that needs to be eaten immediately, we do the teaching first and the cooking second. We usually don't prepare an entire meal since we eat early (11:00 a.m.). We try to select recipes from a variety of different categories: brunch, soup and salad, tea and crepes (both main dish crepes and dessert crepes), pies, a dish for a women's luncheon, a casserole for a family with small children, homemade pizza, stir fry, etc. Choose any recipes that you like. Consider your budget and remember how many women you are feeding each week. We are usually preparing for ten. When we teach the stir fry, we include a nutrition discussion to encourage women to plan healthy food choices for their family.

The cooking mentor's job is the most time-consuming one each week. Before anyone arrives, she has already shopped for the food, cleaned her kitchen, prepared the table, and set out the serving dishes, utensils, pots and pans, etc. We always appoint one mentor who will help her when the teaching time is nearly over. She and the cooking mentor will go to the kitchen, check on the food that has been cooking, put the beverages on the table, and set out all of the necessary items. At the end of the Bible lesson, everyone goes to the table to sample the food and enjoy conversation together.

The teaching mentor is in charge of the teaching time. The young women should have already done their homework before class so they will feel prepared for the discussions. The other mentors have also reviewed the lesson so they can answer questions or give their personal life experiences if necessary.

When they teach, our mentors give an abbreviated version of the lesson from the *Woman of Grace* book. They guide interaction, using both relevant Scriptures and the questions included in the lessons. Some helpful hints for the teaching mentor include:

- Try to involve everyone in the discussion as you teach. If some women are reluctant to speak, they can be asked to read a passage from the Bible. Usually after the first meeting they feel more comfortable and become willing to participate.

- Use the Bible as your source of authority.

- Use questions that relate to their lives.

- Add your own experiences. Sharing your failures encourages them to ask for help and seek counsel for their problems.

- Ask the other mentors to be ready to participate in the conversation or answer a question when no one responds within a minute or two. Often, when one person shares, others are willing to join in, and one comment leads to another.

- Try not to go over the time that has been allotted for the lesson.

- Do your best to cover the entire lesson. Make sure that the women get to answer the questions that are asked in the materials they have studied, otherwise they may feel that it is not important to prepare. Have another mentor tell you when there are ten minutes left in the teaching time, then summarize what remains, and close on time.

One woman commented: "When the mentors teach, it helps us as younger women because we are just beginning this chapter of marriage and raising kids. The mentors apply Titus 2 directly in their lives which is such a great example to us."

After the women leave, all the mentors help clean up. They usually discuss the morning and how the women responded to the lesson. Sometimes one mentor may sense a need in one of the young women and share it with the others. It will be a matter of prayer in the future, and perhaps prompt a follow-up call. When urgent problems arise, a meeting can be set up with one of the mentors.

The last meeting of each session ends with a beautiful banquet. The girls are told to invite their husbands to a special "date night" provided by the mentors for their enjoyment. It is usually held on a weekend evening. The mentors plan the menu, decorate the venue, and prepare all of the food. You will need to choose a home large enough for a sit-down banquet for all your members and husbands. Usually at least two tables are needed to seat everyone. Sometimes we have used the church fellowship hall which also has a large kitchen adjoining it. The evening begins with prayer and food. We often have a photographer (one of the husbands) take pictures of the entire group and the individual couples. The best time to do this is before the food is served. The older women are busy getting the food ready to be served. We ask 3-4 adult volunteers to act as servers for our banquet, freeing the mentors and their husbands to enjoy conversation with the younger couples. It also keeps the mentors from having to leave the table to serve the food, refill glasses, remove the plates from the table, and serve the dessert. Dessert is served with coffee or hot tea. Usually we have at least two options—one chocolate and one non-chocolate. Sometimes we include a fruit selection for diabetics or those who are gluten-free.

After dessert, we engage in a special (and appropriate) form of entertainment—*The Newlywed Game* —where the younger couples compete for a grand prize. It is always fun and creates plenty of laughter.

The game is followed by sharing time. The girls are asked to come prepared to share a special memory from the program, their favorite experience, or a truth that has touched their life. Often the husbands share changes they have observed in their wives and how this has impacted their family or marriage. This is truly a gratifying time for all of the women who have been involved.

We close the evening in prayer. The mentors pray specifically for each young woman, her husband, her family, special needs, upcoming decisions, and wisdom for raising their children. The husbands are often touched by the love and care that has been demonstrated to their wives by the mentors. Usually by the end, tears are shed and sniffles are heard throughout the room. One of the men usually closes the prayer time and final hugs are given as everyone prepares to return home. The mentors stay to clean up and put the rooms back in order before leaving.

Evaluation forms are given to the young women and mentors to fill out and return to the director. They help to determine the program's effectiveness and often give ways to improve it before the next session begins. We have a final meeting as mentors to share the results of the surveys and discuss how to make the program better. We pray one last time for the participants.

~ Finances ~

Before you begin your mentoring ministry, you must establish how it will be financed. The majority of your expenses will come from the food for the weekly meetings and the banquet. Other expenses include study materials for mentors and trainees, childcare (if you don't recruit volunteers), centerpieces, other decor, and prizes for the banquet. Favors for the young women are a wonderful extra touch if you have the time and resources available to do this. You need to consider how you will meet all of these expenses.

If your group is associated with a local church, perhaps it will help defray some of the cost through the church budget. Sometimes you can ask for donations. We are blessed to have mentors who donate the food they use in the demonstrations. They also pay for and prepare the food for the banquet. These mentors consider this part of their hospitality budget and willingly give in this way. Our local church donates the study materials for each young woman and pays for some of the favors for the participants. We keep our expenses minimal by providing free childcare for the children. We begin by recruiting some of the young women who have participated in the program in the past. (We ask on the evaluation forms if our alumni women can help in future programs. One woman was so thrilled with what she had experienced in *Woman of Grace* that she volunteered to babysit for a friend so that she could participate.) Then we recruit other volunteers from the congregation to help.

~ Favors ~

The favors we supply are usually associated with the lesson taught on that day. Here are some we have used:

- Keepers at Home – *aprons, recipe cards, a book on organizing their home or their schedule*
- Kindness – *handmade notecards (to be used to thank someone for kindness shown to them)*

- Loving Husbands – *a book on the subject, candle holders and candles to prepare for a special evening, and chocolates*

- Loving Children – *a book on the subject, a special toy for the children, homemade "play dough" with cookie cutters included*

- Purity – *a beautiful, fragrant bar of soap, or skincare lotion*

- Submission – *a devotional book or a journal*

- Hospitality – *guest room baskets, a cookie press for baking, other small gadgets used in the kitchen*

Use your imagination and your available finances. These little gifts don't have to be expensive, just thoughtful. Submission is the most difficult lesson for which to find a gift. Since it is also often the most difficult lesson for the young women, we usually supply them with a devotional book to aid them in their walk with the Lord. If the gifts are small, we put them on the dining table. If they are larger, we give them to the women as they leave.

In closing, remember that every group should tailor it to their own needs. Work with what you have. Try different ways to accomplish the basic goals of the program. Pray for God to give you the ideas that will work with your women. Use whatever resources He gives. Trust Him to work in the hearts of those you mentor and bring His eternal results.

~ One Woman's Experience ~

"This program has changed my life and was one of the best things that ever happened to me. It changed my attitude toward my family, and made me realize they are worth the effort! I discovered that my family deserved a home that was clean, and they deserved to know where their clean clothes were. I stopped thinking of those things as chores that *had* to be done, and started thinking of them as ways I could bless my family. I found that by making time to give my husband and children a well-run home, that suddenly I had more time to do the fun things. In my case, I chose to spend one day each week *to do it all*. I think also realizing that other women had struggled with all the topics we discussed helped me feel more like I could face my faults and deal with them."

~ Conversation Questions ~

These questions are designed to stimulate discussion and application. The mentor should print them (or prepare her own) and distribute them during the meal time each week. Go around the table and give each woman the opportunity to answer and to add their own comments and questions. This can be a helpful culmination of the lesson, transforming truth into practice. It is often a time of heart-warming conviction, repentance, and resolution to obey the commands of Scripture as the Holy Spirit moves among His people.

Christ Calls Us to Keep Our Homes

1. What is your greatest challenge in keeping your home clean and orderly?

2. What chores around the house are appropriate for small children to accomplish?

3. How can you minister to your husband this week as a home manager?

4.   What is the most difficult thing for you to accomplish in meal preparation and planning?

5.   Do you have a family budget? What system do you use to track all of your expenses?

Christ Calls Us to Kindness

1.   What are specific ways that we may carry each other's burdens through kindness?

2.   How have others carried your burdens through kindness?

3.   How do you model *treating others the way you want to be treated* to your children?

4.   How is God glorified through our acts of kindness? Why is it important to consider this?

Christ Calls Us to Love Our Husbands

1.   Do you know how to really bless your husband? Encouraging words, acts of service, gifts, touching, quality time, which of these really says "I love you!" to him?

2.   What is one chore your husband dreads? Is there a good reason you couldn't do it for him?

3.   Is it ever right to withhold sex from your husband?

4.   What is one thing you can do for fun with your husband? Go test drive a car he will never buy? Try to climb a mountain with him? Go to the shooting range and learn to shoot his gun? Give him a foot massage? Go camping, even if you aren't a camper?

5.   What steps can you take now to foster companionship and friendship with your husband? What new hobby could you try?

6.   How may you comfort your husband when he is sick?

Christ Calls Us to Love Our Children

1.   Do you pray regularly for your children? What do you pray for them?

2.   Do you and your husband agree on the methods of discipline? Have you had to make any compromises in this area?

3.   In a time when your child may be discouraged, what is one way you can show that you love and cherish him or her?

4.   We mentioned in this lesson that our children belong to the Lord. How would you respond if your child decided to spend his life serving God on the mission field (or move to another state)? How *should* you respond?

5.   What are some of the good qualities that you find in each of your children? How are they different from one another?

6.   What is the most difficult thing for you in disciplining your children?

7.   If you do not have children, what are some qualities or character traits that you would want to instill in your children if you had them?

8.   When you were growing up, what kind of discipline did your parents practice? Would you do the same things with your children?

Christ Calls Us to Purity

1. What are some rewards of living a life of purity?

2. In what ways do you model purity to your children?

3. What are some practical ways you and your husband set standards for dress, TV, movies, books, Internet, and other cultural influences?

4. Do you consider flirting to be sinful?

5. Purity involves making hard choices. Our culture is steeped in self-centeredness and "my rights." There are no boundaries. When do you feel the most vulnerable to temptation in this area?

6. How do busyness, tiredness, selfishness, insecurity, and loneliness play into your temptations?

7. Are you and your husband comfortable talking about purity and sexual issues?

Christ Calls Us to Submit to Our Husbands

1. How you got along with your father will determine, in part, how you get along with your husband. Did you submit to your dad's authority? Explain.

2. Was submission modeled by your mother as you were growing up?

3. Some say the biggest issues to deal with in marriage are money, in-laws, or raising children. In what areas do you struggle most with submission?

4. How does submitting to your husband impact the spread of the gospel message?

5. How do you and your husband make financial decisions? How are spending decisions related to submission?

6. What if you are naturally better than your husband at doing something like balancing the checkbook, leading family devotions, or doing household repairs? Does it really matter who takes the lead in these things?

Christ Calls Us to Hospitality

1. For the stage of life that you are presently in, what is the best way for you to demonstrate hospitality?

2. Are there specific persons or types of persons that God has laid upon your heart to invite into your home?

3. What is the most difficult obstacle for you in practicing hospitality?

4. Do you regularly have guests in your home for meals, desserts, coffee, or overnight?

5. What is your favorite way to show hospitality?

6. How could you use your home for:

   A. Outreach to your unsaved friends or neighbors?

   B. Ministry to Christian friends?

7. Practicing hospitality is not always convenient. What can you do to be prepared for the unexpected?

8. Are there ways to show hospitality besides having guests in your home?

9. Has this lesson changed how you view hospitality? How?

Notes

1. Susan Hunt, *Spiritual Mothering* (Wheaton, IL: Crossway Books, 1992), p. 42.

2. Susan Hunt, *Spiritual Mothering* (Wheaton, IL: Crossway Books, 1992), p. 136.

3. Donna Otto, *Between Women of God* (Eugene, OR: Harvest House Publisher, 1995), pp. 174-176.

4. Donna Otto, *Finding a Mentor, Being a* Mentor (Eugene, OR: Harvest House Publisher, 2001), pp. 136-137.

5. Donna Otto, *Between Women of God* (Eugene, OR: Harvest House Publisher, 1995), pp. 19-20.

6. Vickie Kraft, *The Influential Woman* (Dallas, TX: Thomas Nelson, 1992), pp. 29-30.

7. Susan Hunt, *Spiritual Mothering* (Wheaton, IL: Crossway Books, 1992), p. 51.

8. Donna Otto, *Between Women of God* (Eugene, OR: Harvest House Publisher, 1995), p. 177.

9. Donna Otto, *Finding a Mentor, Being a* Mentor (Eugene, OR: Harvest House Publisher, 2001), pp. 137-138.

10. Jon Mohr, *Find Us Faithful,* Copyright 1988 by Birdwing Music/Jonathan Mark Music.

Suggested Resources

Kraft, Vickie. *Women Mentoring Women*. Chicago,IL: Moody Press, 1992.

George, Elizabeth. *A Woman's High Calling*. Eugene, OR: Harvest House Publishers, 2001.

Peace, Martha. *Becoming a Titus 2 Woman*. Focus Publishing, 1997.

Peace, Martha. *The Excellent Wife*. Focus Publishing, 1995.

Made in the USA
Las Vegas, NV
15 January 2024

84409329R00077